# PRINCIPLES AND PRACTICE OF
# THE RORSCHACH PERSONALITY TEST

*W. Mons*

★

M.R.C.S., L.R.C.P., Lt.-Col. R.A.M.C., Adviser in Psychiatry, S.E.A.C., Late consultant Psychologist, Cornwall County Education Committee, Hon. Psychotherapist, Cornwall County Mental Hospital, etc.

# PRINCIPLES AND PRACTICE OF
# THE RORSCHACH PERSONALITY TEST

by

## W. MONS

FABER AND FABER LIMITED
24 Russell Square
London

*First published in mcmxlvii
by Faber and Faber Limited
24 Russell Square London W.C.1
Printed in Great Britain by
Latimer Trend & Co Ltd Plymouth*

# PREFACE

When I first started experimenting with the Rorschach ink blot test ten years ago I went through a hard school of trial and error. At that time I had already a good many excellent publications on the subject to guide me, the fruits of earnest and painstaking research by experienced psychologists. I fondly hoped to become an expert myself by collecting information from the works of others, thus accumulating a store of principles and formulae which should enable me to apply the test in practice like an empirically standardized instrument.

But I was to discover that neither standards nor conceptions had any uniformity of character, and that even within the various schools, the individual workers permitted themselves a considerable amount of freedom in their definitions and interpretations. I realized that, unless every response were fully understood in its significance for the particular person being tested, a reliable and clear personality picture could not be hoped for.

It was my good fortune some years ago to be given an opportunity to undertake a systematic study of the method and its significance, when I had the honour of being consultant psychologist to a progressive County Education Committee who visualized the significance of this work, and allowed me every facility to carry on my research. The result was a collection of over a thousand selected records of children and adolescents from the age of four to sixteen. One half of these was provided by hostels, remand homes and institutions, and represented abnormal conditions of special clinical interest to the psychologist: delinquents and problem children, enuretics, air raid neuroses, mental defectives and a group of organic invalidism. The schools supplied the other half as a control group which was divided into an equal number of boys and girls for each year of age. These were chosen on grounds of medical fitness and freedom from neurotic traits, a uniformity of social background and an I.Q. between 90 and 105. Both groups were tested by the Terman-Merril modification of The Stanford-Binet Test or the Kent Oral Method, and teachers and welfare workers co-operated freely in supplying any relevant information that was beyond my reach.

This study will form the subject of a special publication in the near future. Here it merely serves as the basis for certain theories and explanations which should enable the reader to understand the rationale of the test. The child being father of the man, it is not surprising that this experience with children opened up a better understanding of many adult problems. It was found particularly helpful in assessing the personalities of the psychiatric battle casualties that passed through our hospital during the North-European Campaign, because 200 of the soldiers tested belonged to the same social and educational group as those children, matured by age and experience, confronted with unexpected problems, and reacting to their difficulties as could have been predicted.

It is hoped that these investigations will have achieved the purpose of enabling me to give a satisfactory explanation for all the factors of the test. My aim is freedom from dogmatism where the method is concerned, and its reduction to a basis of logic and common sense. If I fall short of this ambition in a good many places, it is due to the fact that I am compiling this little book in the field from my lectures, having neither textbooks at hand nor even access to my notes stored in England. Brigadier J. R. Rees, Consultant Psychiatrist to the Army, and my Commanding Officers were kind enough to suggest that I should give a few lectures on the Rorschach Method, and the response to these has been so gratifying that I willingly acceded to the request to publish some introductions for beginners.

It is not intended that this book should take the place of its betters, but that it should serve as an introduction for the study of more advanced works.[1] The methods adopted are based on those suggested

---

[1] See in particular: Klopfer, B. and Kelley, D. McG. *The Rorschach Technique, a Manual for a Projective Method of Personality Diagnosis.* World Book Co., New York and London, 1942.

# Preface

by the Rorschach Institute in the pages of the *Rorschach Research Exchange*[1] so admirably edited by Klopfer. The works of Beck[2] and of Binder[3] have also been incorporated, and where some criticism has been ventured or alterations suggested, this had only been done after well over a thousand records had been examined for those points. The pioneer work of Rorschach[4] and of Oberholzer[5] has naturally been fundamental in all these studies. To these and to a great many other important publications[6] the reader is referred for his further progress. In them he will find detailed accounts of the test findings in almost any clinical condition, and for this reason the diagnostic side has purposely been left here in the state of a sketchy outline.

Only a few diagnostic addenda have been made as points of interest. It is felt that an understanding of the mechanism of the test will enable every experienced psychiatrist to form a valid conclusion, and that the subject of specific clinical conditions does not come within the framework of this modest outline of the principles.

[1] *Rorschach Research Exchange*, published by Rorschach Institute Inc., edited by Bruno Klopfer.

[2] Beck, S. T. 'Introduction to the Rorschach Method. A Manual of Personality Study.' *Amer, J. Orthopsychiat. Assn. Monograph, 1937*, Vol. I, pp. xv–278. Since published in book form.

[3] Binder, H. 'Comments concerning the Beck-Klopfer Discussion. '*Ror. Res. Exch, 1937*, Vol. II, pp. 43–4.

'Shading Responses in Rorschach Reactions' (in German). *Schweiz. Arch. Neurol. Psychiat., 1932–3*, Vol. XXX, pp. 1–67 and 233–86. Reprinted Orel Fussli, Zürich, 1932.

'The Light-Dark Interpretations in Rorschach's Experiment.' *Ror. Res. Exch., 1937*, Vol. II, pp. 37–42.

*Id et alia.* 'Discussion on some Recent Rorschach Problems.' Ibid., pp. 43–72.

[4] Rorschach, H. *Psychodiagnostik*. 4th Ed., 1941. Engl. Transl. Hans Huber, Berne, 1942.

[5] *Idem et* Oberholzer, E. 'Zur Auswertung des Formdeutversuchs für die Psychoanalyse.' *Z. Ges. Neurol. Psychiat., 1923*, Vol. LXXXII, pp. 240–74. Also translated as 'The Application of the Interpretation of Form to Psychoanalysis.' *J. Nerv. Ment. Dis., 1924*, Vol. LX, pp. 225–48 and 359–79.

[6] An excellent bibliography is appended to the Manual of Klopfer and Kelley, and Oberholzer is bringing his index up to date annually. The *Rorschach Research Exchange* is, of course, the most important American periodical for the Rorschach worker, but he should also consult the *Amer. J. Orthopsychiat.* and the *Amer. J. Gen. Psychol.* for the latest publications. See also Rapaport, D., *Diagnostic Psychological Testing*, Vol. II, pp. 85–394. The Year Book Publishers, Inc., Chicago, 1946.

## Preface

I wish to express my sincere gratitude to Dr. G. S. Nightingale, without whose untiring assistance and keen criticism these pages would not have been completed, and to Dr. C. J. C. Earl, who, though in poor health, found time to add most valuable comments and suggestions.

W.M.

# CONTENTS

PREFACE                                                          *page* 5

## 1
## THE THEORY OF THE TEST                                        13

## 2
## THE PRACTICE OF THE TEST                                      21

The record sheet                                                22
The administration of the test                                  23
The enquiry                                                      26

## 3
## SCORING AND TABULATION                                        30

THE MENTAL APPROACH :
  $W$, $\text{W}$, $D$, $d$, $dd$, $ddd$, and $S$ responses    30

PERSONALITY STRUCTURE :
  Movement responses : $m$, $FM$ and $M$                      38
  Chiaroscuro responses : $K$, $k$, $FK$                      39
  Pure Form responses : $F$, $F$, $+$ $F-$                    40
  The Surface Texture responses : $Fc$, $cF$, $c$             41
  The Black and White Colour responses : $FC'$, $C'F$, $C'$   42
  The Colour responses : $FC$, $CF$, and $C$                  42

THE CONTENT :                                                   43
  Animal responses                                           43
  Human figure responses                                     44
  Ordinary responses                                         44
  Pathognomic responses                                      44

9

# Contents

QUANTITY AND QUALITY OF THE RESPONSES *page* 45
 The Distribution of the responses 45
 The Popular responses, *P* 45
 The original response, *O* 45
 The average time 46
 The time for the first response 46
 The additional responses 46

THE CHARACTER OF THE RESPONSE 46
 Confabulation 46
 Morbidity 46
 Schizoid trend 47
 Remarks 47
 Exclamation 47
 Question form 47
 Sexual 47
 Rejections 47
 Turning 48

THE LAST-3-CARDS % 49

THE TABULATION OF PERCENTAGES 49

DIAGRAM OF TABULATION SHEET 51–55

## 4

## THE SIGNIFICANCE OF THE SEPARATE SCORES 56

THE MENTAL APPROACH
 Significance of *W*, *W̶*, *D*, *d*, *dd*, *ddd*, and *S* responses 56

THE PERSONALITY STRUCTURE 61
 Significance of the movement responses *m*, *FM* & *M* 61
 Significance of *K*, *k*, and *FK* 66
 Significance of *F*, *F+* and F − 69
 Significance of the Surface-texture responses *Fc*, *cF*, and *c*. 76
 Significance of the pseudo-colour responses, black and white, *C'* 77
 Significance of the colour responses, *FC*, *CF* and *C* 78

THE SIGNIFICANCE OF THE CONTENT 80
 Animal responses 80
 Anatomy responses 80
 Responses of 'blood' and 'fire' 82

10

# Contents

FACTORS RELATING TO QUALITY AND QUANTITY OF
RESPONSES *page* 83
The number of responses and the Percentage of the
last 3 Cards 83
The significance of *P* 83
The significance of *O* 83
The significance of the average time 84
The significance of the time lapse for the first response 84
The additional responses 85

THE SIGNIFICANCE OF THE CHARACTER OF THE RESPONSE 85
The significance of Confabulation 85
. Morbid trends 85
the Schizoid response 86
the remarks and exclamations 87
the question form of response 87
sexual trends in the response 87
Rejections 88
the turning of the cards 89

5

## THE ASSESSMENT OF THE PERSONALITY 90

SCOPE AND PLAN OF PROCEDURE. RELATIONSHIPS 92
The Basic Personality and the Graph 93
Mental Activity 94
(a) The Mental Approach 94
(b) The $W:M$ and $W: (m+FM+M+K)$ 97
The Intellectual Level 98
The Emotional Life 105
(a) Ties with outer reality 105
(b) Ties with the inner life 107
Vocational Advice from the Basic Personality 108
Other factors for integration into the personality picture 110
Abnormal features of the record and their assessment 111
(a) Abnormalities of the Personality structure 112
(b) Abnormalities of the Content 113
(c) Abnormal character of the response 113
(d) Remarks, exclamations, rejections 114
(e) $(A+H): (Ad+Hd)$ 114

11

# Contents

(f) Special formulae for diagnostic purposes     *page* 115

    (1) Signs of Colour Shock     115

    (2) Signs of Neurosis     118

    (3) Signs of Hysteria     119

    (4) Signs of Organic Lesion     119

The Analysis of the content     126

## 6

## SOME USEFUL ELABORATIONS OF THE METHOD  123

ADDITIONS TO THE MENTAL APPROACH. THE $Wv$     123

BECK'S 'ORGANIZING TALENT', $z$     124

ENLARGEMENTS OF THE PERSONALITY STRUCTURE     125

    (a) $Mm$ responses     125

    (b) $Km$ and $Cm$     126

    (c) Difficult forms of $K$, $KF$, $F/K$ & $K/F$     127

    (d) $F/C$ and $C/F$     127

    (e) $C$ symbolic     128

    (f) $Cc$ and $CK$     128

    (g) The position response, $Po$     129

ADDITIONS TO THE CONTENT     130

    (a) $Hdx$ and $Adx$     130

ADDITIONAL RELATIONSHIPS     131

    (a) $(m+FM) : (K+k+FK)$     131

    (b) $(\Sigma K+k+FK) : (\Sigma c+\Sigma C') -$     132

## 7

## SOME DIAGNOSTIC ADDENDA     133

THE 'NORMAL' PERSONALITY IN FACT AND IN RECORD     133

NEUROSES, PSYCHOSES, AND MENTAL DEFECT     135

OTHER CONDITIONS : EPILEPSY, ENURESIS, AND JUVENILE
DELINQUENCY     136

## 8

EXAMPLES     142

INDEX     159

# I

# THE THEORY OF THE TEST

What does the Rorschach ink blot test measure? It does not 'measure' anything so much as reveal qualities. In contrast with intelligence, aptitude, memory and similar tests which try to assess quantitatively, the aim of the Rorschach is to give an impression of the total personality as a structure composed of many parts and pieces. In a similar way, the word-association test or the picture-description method probe the personality, but only a very limited part of it, because they are based on concrete concepts— definite words or definite pictures.

Other books will tell of the origin of the idea of using blots of ink to elicit responses, an idea going back to the last century[1]; here we can only briefly honour the memory of the young Swiss psychiatrist, Rorschach, whose genius put the method on a working basis from which our modern system has developed. By squashing Indian ink and liquid stains or dyes between a folded sheet of paper, Rorschach made ink blot pictures which he asked his psychotics to name; he discovered that the answer received bore a close relationship to the type of illness. He began to use several series of such blots on several series of patients, and finally selected the present range of ten cards (of which we use facsimiles).

The first thing that struck him was the patient's attitude to colour; while a black or grey blot would be more or less rationally interpreted as form, colour evoked an undoubtedly emotional reaction. Form would time and again be ignored, and a similarity be sought in colour only. That this was indeed an emotional reaction was easily proved

[1] Simon H. Tulchin, Ph.B.: 'The Pre-Rorschach use of Ink Blot Tests.' *Rorschach Res. Exch., Jan. 1940*, pp. 1–7.

by the clinical picture of the patient as well as by the fact that 'normal' people always blended colour with form. The emotional personality—not necessarily the emotionally unstable only—is one who derives pleasure from sun and flowers, from congenial coloration of the environment, a personality who is 'extratensive', to use the classical term, living essentially in his outer surroundings actively or passively, one who 'does things' by preference to thinking or reading about them, who looks to the outer world for inspiration, guidance and enjoyment.

The second factor that came to light was a process of imagination which not only produced 'form' but animated it with movement. While the colour response, for instance, a blue blot seen as a patch of sky, had come mainly from elated manics, the movement response, such as 'a running man', occurred mainly in the depressives. We know that in this depressed phase the patient visibly slows his activities, that he becomes lethargic and shuns movement, and sits brooding; phantasy of movement has taken the place of activity. ('introvert' type of personality.)

Between these two extremes of the scale fall the responses which are inspired purely by the shape and the outline of the blot. This is a process of reason, of intellect based neither on an emotional reaction to colour nor on a stimulated phantasy which creates a story. For movement, however short, is linked to a time factor and shows a part of a story, of an action. Pure form is a mechanical translation of the picture symbol into a word symbol. The 'fighting dog' of the depressive becomes merely 'a dog', possibly elaborated in detail and classified as to its breed, but the idea of motion does not arise. Similarly, the manic's 'blue sky' has now become an 'insect' or any other object of which its form is reminiscent, irrespective of its colour, which may be totally inappropriate.

Soon it was discovered that there were many other kinds of response to the blots, as well as many combinations, and their incidence correlated with the clinical picture of the person under test. As the experience became larger and more comprehensive, a great many factors came to light, which all had significance in the make-up of human personality, and it was finally realized that the Rorschach method allowed the most comprehensive insight of any method yet devised into the structure of the personality.

When one considers the many-sidedness of human nature, one will also understand why any attempt at simplification of the test must

14

needs lead to a defeat of our own aim to get a comprehensive insight into a personality. The Rorschach Test has often been described as 'time wasting' and 'cumbersome', but when we reflect on the time it takes to get to know another person so well that we are no longer deceived by the outer personality, the expenditure of a few hours' work does not seem excessive.

It obviously is not the method of choice if we are sure of the clinical picture, or if the quest is a trifling one, but, where grave doubt exists, or where we are asked to advise on momentous problems, the test will in most cases give us the right answer.

It may not give us invariably the answer we are looking for or expecting, nor can we claim that it will always satisfy our curiosity. Our task will always be to interpret correctly whatever results the test has produced and to add the result to our impression of the clinical picture.

The Rorschach Test is not a mechanical device which will automatically produce the correct diagnosis[1]; it must be used as a delicate instrument which must be adjusted to the requirements of certain groups of cases; not of the individual, but of the group to which that individual belongs. Age, sex, education, intelligence level and race, are some of the major groups one has to consider. For instance, all average British boys of the age of nine years can be compared according to the same standards, but it would lead to gross errors to apply these standards to the record of a neurotic Polish lady of forty-nine. We cannot get more out of the test than we put in. Its results depend on our own insight into the workings of human nature, and a thorough understanding of the significance of each detail of the test. By now, some three hundred books on the test have been published, apart from countless treatises in periodicals and a paper of its own, *The Rorschach Exchange Research*. Already a host of conflicting theories have taken the battlefield, and heavy guns are firing in all directions confusing symbols based both on different languages and on diverging conceptions. If the test is not to lose its value in this Babelian battle we have to establish fundamental principles which can be checked by any experimenter, and lay a foundation of common sense upon which to build up theories and practices.

It is claimed that these ink blots constitute a Personality Test; it

[1] It does not produce a diagnostic 'label', instead it gives a picture of the make-up of a personality, from which, dependent on his knowledge of psychology, the examiner can deduce the clinical condition.

does not profess to predict the future. It aims at revealing as many sides of the personality as the record, the patient's response series, will allow. It tries to show the inner make-up, the human mechanism, and it remains with the psychiatrist to integrate these data into conjectures of likely behaviour. To the layman, a motor car is a conveyance of relative comfort; to the expert, each type has structural advantages for different specific purposes of use. Of the human machine we want to know its strong points and its weaknesses, its talents and its failings, its driving powers and their utilization. Intelligence is only an integral part of the total personality, and if we want to get nothing but an I.Q. we have quicker and more accurate tests to hand than the Rorschach. We want to know something of the person's own mental ability, the quality of his phantasy processes by which he transforms experience into behaviour, theory into practical concept, and imagination into work and creation. We want to look into his emotional life to see how it affects his inner life and development, how it influences his outer existence and his attitude towards his environment. We would like to know whether he is practical, or a theorist; creative or analytical. We would like to find out as much as possible about his character and habits—is he orderly, methodical, or negligent; is he easily influenced, is he uncertain of himself, or is he arrogant and domineering? Is he liable to become, for instance, a chronic delinquent under certain circumstances? Has he freely developed since childhood, or is he still wearing his baby shoes? Has he unfolded all his talents to the full, or are there dormant and unsuspected gifts that await awakening? What are his potentialities?

All this, and many side-lines, apply equally well to the normal and to the abnormal. It is when these questions have been answered that we start casting about for signs of grosser abnormality, of upsets in the personality, of possible mental illness. Each mental illness has its own characteristic symptoms, and these will affect the patient's reactions to the ink blots in characteristic ways. Just as behaviour pattern and phantasy content vary clinically, so does the result of the test show the failings of the mind that deals with the task. The more it is a question of mental and emotional qualities, the clearer does the test answer our question. An early schizophrenia, for instance, can usually be suspected, while an appendicitis will escape detection.

It is possible to make a correct diagnosis from a clear and satisfactory test record alone, provided one is informed of the main groups to which the patient belongs. But it is not possible generally to say from the record alone whether it belongs to a patient proper or a member of the general public at large, though no doubt such a distinction can sometimes be made. What we are dealing with are personality potentials. Under favourable circumstances a very unusual or abnormal personality may go through life without breakdown or mishap; under unwarranted stress a mild deviation from the normal average will be enough to lead to a breakdown according to predisposition. What we are diagnosing are personality patterns, and our experience in psychology must tell us how these would react to any given situation. In practice we are usually consulted when that situation has arisen and the breakdown has resulted. The symptoms will then tally with the pattern of the personality and its predispositions. The war has shown us that some men with an apparently heavy predisposition to neurotic breakdown can go through several campaigns before reaching their limit, while others appear to break down in the first few days of battle with only a moderate predisposition. We cannot predict the circumstances which will approach one man and cause his collapse through their violence and suddenness, nor by what means another has managed to escape a breakdown.

We must remember that what is 'normal' under one set of circumstances may be 'abnormal' under another. A creative artist or an inspired writer will give responses that in a bricklayer would be signs of abnormality. Unless he be judged by neurotic standards, a nervous child with an I.Q. of well over 100 may give responses similar to those given by mental defectives. In all cases one should always be in possession of the essential factors before making a diagnosis, and in particular it should be stressed that one should be informed whether the person in question is a member of the community at large or a patient in, for instance, a Mental Hospital. Neglect of this precaution can otherwise lead to socially embarrassing situations, as in the case of a young Rorschach worker who practised 'blind' diagnosis and wrote 'Schizophrenic with Homicidal tendencies' underneath the anonymous record of his Superintendent; this method is so informative that one should never test one's friends or colleagues.

## THE TEST MATERIAL[1]

The test material consists of ten standardized ink blots, which have been selected carefully from a considerable series of such blots. They

[1] See diagrams, pp. 31–34.

were originally made by dropping ink or colour on a white sheet and creating a good impression of symmetry by squashing it after folding. Each card has a 'Primary position', the easiest way of holding it to 'see something in it' and on its back, printed in one corner, is the number it takes in the series so that it can be identified and placed as intended. The sequence of the cards has been given special thought, and the character of each stands in relation to its precursor and successor. Card I has many form possibilities, while the chiaroscuro, the shading from black to grey, is not disturbing; it is the most suitable for acquainting the patient with his task. Card II unexpectedly introduces a bright Red with the black just when the patient thought he knew what he would have to look at. Card III becomes more disrupted in design, more difficult to interpret as one whole picture. Card IV has discarded all colour, but intensified the black and contracted the shape, while Card V is the most circumscribed and also the darkest in colour of all. Card VI develops shadings of grey within a shape that does not lend itself to easy interpretation. Card VII is a scattering of light-grey shapes giving readily an impression of vague outline. Then appears unexpectedly the first of the three all-colour cards, and the beholder must make a rapid adjustment of his method of interpretation. He can deliberately (if unconsciously) ignore colour, or try to blend it with form. He will undergo a certain emotional stress, unless he be completely obtuse to environmental colour. Card IX is less pleasing in design and colour scheme than its predecessor, and therefore makes the task more difficult, both from the intellectual and from the emotional point of view. Finally, in Card X, comes a riot of colour with a complete breaking up of harmonious form into separate blots which make a 'whole blot response' extremely difficult, and the emotional component very powerful—either helping or hindering the task.

As the patient looks at each card in turn and gives his interpretation of what he sees, he is forced to go through a mental and emotional process which shapes his responses. The blots are so vague that they allow for a free play of imagination, thousands of different pictures can be seen in each card, though certain more or less stereotyped interpretations will predominate and be somewhat characteristic of each. But the fact that 'no two people see alike' is strikingly illustrated by results, for among the records of two thousand people, no two are identical. The powers that set the human machine in motion dictate the trend of the responses; from instinct-driven infancy, experience, both intrinsic and extraneous, has shaped man's mental and physical development, his personality; understanding takes the place of wonderment, reason governs desire, self-control the emotions. Behaviour patterns develop, trends come to the fore, impressions leave their stamp. Experience has moulded the inherent qualities to a personality. This personality must always have an harmonious total structure both in life and in the Rorschach result. Contrasts will appear, but not contradictions. The record of an 'idiot savant' will always be that of mental defective, the record of a chronic neurotic will always reveal abnormality, that of the labourer differ from that of the 'Varsity man. Deliberate falsification of responses on the part of the patient destroys that harmony of the individual personality structure and arouses suspicion at once, particularly when we can compare the test result with the clinical picture. The malingerer cannot help giving himself away in so involved a test as this, where he does not know in the least what one is looking for. If he performs as he should, he will fail to give indications of illness, if he takes refuge in a few guarded responses he arouses suspicion, the more so if his performance is grossly at variance with what one would expect from his type of personality.

That the record of each individual personality is characteristic can be demonstrated by a series of re-tests after a number of years, or every six to twelve months. It is not surprising that one gets very similar responses when the test is repeated within a few days. But it is surprising to be able to identify a definite personality from a series of records, to enucleate the basic personality, as it were, and follow the developments of the total personality through the years. Experience shapes and matures, it develops and restrains, but the fundamental personality remains. It is also curious how certain unusual responses return again and again after six, twelve, or more months. Sometimes the person will remember the earlier impression and exclaim, 'Oh, here is the (So-and-so) again: I remember it.' At other times a person may believe he has produced a new response entirely, yet a comparison with the earlier record shows that it was merely forgotten. On the average some 25–30 per cent of the responses are identical or similar on second test after a year, and at least half of those are unusual ones. Another interesting side-light comes from testing uniovular twins, where frequently a 50 per cent agreement occurs in the individual responses, while the final result will show the essential differences in personality structure.

19

# The Rorschach Test

Re-tests have been taken after a five-years' interval, when it could be safely assumed that the original answers had been forgotten. Yet in every case the final interpretation revealed still the same person, only maturer by the experiences of time, or else regressed or otherwise affected—showing, in other words, the wear and tear of the years but still the same individuality. We may therefore discard all doubt about the significance of the test: there is nothing haphazard or accidental about it, as might at first glance appear. The conscious, voluntary reactions involved are less important than the host of unconscious, automatic ones, which the relative speed of the test, the element of surprise, and the directed attention will not allow the patient to put under control. The Rorschach test fulfils its claim as a method of probing human personality.

# 2

---

## THE PRACTICE OF THE TEST

---

When I first attempted to learn to handle the Rorschach Test ten years ago, I had two very excellent books on the method to guide me. Nevertheless I wasted a good deal of time on trial and error, because it all seemed so complicated, and I was searching in vain for such 'hints for beginners' as would have assisted my ignorance. I therefore venture to suggest a few points as an introduction to the actual practice of the test.

It is a great help to get to know the blots fairly well before starting to apply the test to others. An hour or two spent on 'testing' oneself is an excellent investment. For this purpose the cards are placed in order face down in a pile with Card I on top, and examined one by one, the ideas suggested by the blots being put down in writing. The most suitable paper for the record is closely ruled foolscap, about 45–50 lines per sheet, if possible with a margin on either side. If such margined paper is not obtainable, a line should be drawn about ¾ inch from the left-hand edge, and another about 1¼–1½ inches from the right. Each card should be looked at in its standard position first —as indicated by the print on the back, and then turned as desired, till all the possibilities suggested by the blot are exhausted. Anything that looks like something can qualify as an interpretation. This first unbiased attempt has almost the same value as a clinical test and can later be assessed. For this purpose it will be necessary to make a note identifying the part of the blot evoking each idea or 'response'. In the case of such a 'self-test' it will probably be found sufficient to refer in broad terms to quadrants, or 'spikes' along certain edges,

21

when the blot is not interpreted as a whole. It will be found helpful for future tests to refer to 'upper' and 'lower' parts of the blot always in the standard position. For instance the two red blots on Cards II and III will always be 'upper red' in whatever position the card is held. The actual position of the card is recorded on the score sheet with the symbols ∧, ∨, <, >,—the apex pointing out the upper edge of the card. When it is desired to add the scoring to this first test at a later date, each response can easily be identified with the part of the blot in question and the proper scoring can be arrived at.

This initial exercise not only helps to fix the character of each blot in one's memory, but gives one an idea what to expect from others one will test later.

The following extract of a record sheet indicates the main points:

| 162 | *Pte. Smith, H., Pnr. Corps, age 38* | 23 Aug. 45 |
|---|---|---|
| | I. $11^{35}$ | |
| 1.  12″ | ∧∨∧  Looks like a bat to me, sir | *WF A P* |
| 2. | ∨  Could be a map or something | *WF—Map* |
| 3.     + | ∧>∨∧  Looks like the head of a fowl here (Upper lat, corner) | *dF Ad* |
| | ∧  Nothing else I can make out, sir | |
| | $11^{38}$ | |
| | II. | |

The heading contains the serial number of the record for filing purposes in the left-hand margin, obviously only for personal requirements. Then the patient's name, occupation and age. The record of a labourer approaching middle age, for instance, has a characteristic simplicity which would be surprising in that of a medical student. Such a reminder of the group to which the patient belongs will be found helpful. In the right-hand margin goes the date, and the time at which the patient received the first card is noted.

The responses are numbered serially for each card in the left-hand margin, where also the reaction time for the first response to each card is recorded. This time is taken in seconds from the moment the patient is handed the card to the moment he starts giving his first response. Here remarks or exclamations do not count as responses. There is no need to take the time for the subsequent answers to that same card, but where an unusually long period of silence has occurred before another response, a cross, or several crosses if necessary, are sometimes put in the left-hand margin as a reminder, in case one feels the need to explore further such blocking later on.

22

## The Practice of the Test

Between the margins the responses are written down verbatim, preceded by the indication of the position in which the card was held. This is a record of the amount of turning that has taken place and is of significance. It should therefore not be omitted. A note about which part of the blot the response refers to should also be added, especially if the scoring is to be done after the sitting, since size of the blot, its character and colour, enter into the scoring.

In the right-hand margin goes the scoring:

1. Whether the response refers to the whole blot or to part of it.
2. What character of the blot has inspired the response: whether purely form and outline, whether shading, whether the impression of movement, or whether the colour.
3. A coded summary of the content of the response.
4. A note about its quality, whether stereotyped or common, popular, or whether uncommon and original. Other symbols about the quality of the content can be used according to requirements and to facilitate tabulation.

It is clear from this description that the beginner cannot be expected to work out the scoring while taking down the responses. And in many cases of fast-responding individuals even the expert's pen cannot keep pace. Some Rorschach exponents advise shorthand, and this would certainly be of advantage in many instances. I myself have always managed with longhand and the help of abbreviations reminiscent of an estate agent's advertisement. In order to become familiar with the test it is advisable to leave the right-hand margin blank for the first ten or twenty records, or at the most fill in (1). This will permit a certain leisure in which to observe the patient's behaviour and general attitude towards the test.

Exclamations, remarks, comments on colour or other technicalities, and relevant questions, should be noted. They may indicate emotional upsets based on association of ideas not expressed as a proper response, or an attempt to temporize and delay, or express some peculiar attitude which forms one of the many facets of the personality.　　　　　　　　　　　　　—

For taking a patient's record the following procedure is suggested:

One's requirements of margined foolscap having been placed in readiness, the test cards are piled face down within easy reach, and a watch or clock with a second-hand put where the eye can read it without effort, yet hidden from the patient.

The latter should be seated either to the right or the left of the

23

table in a comfortable chair with his back slightly towards the tester who can see the card over the patient's shoulder. This position has the advantage that the patient does not see what is being written and feels more at ease than when he is aware that every word he says is being taken down in writing.

The light should be good without being glaring or sunny. Artificial light changes the colour effects and is therefore unsuitable. A good quality daylight lamp can be used if necessary.

The patient is introduced to his task by some simple formula which should not vary once one is satisfied that it contains all the essentials to set the test in motion. The test is based on the patient's unguided approach and reaction to the ink blots, his free and spontaneous associations. The instructions must therefore leave him as much freedom as possible, and contain no suggestions which might affect his responses. If it seems likely that the patient does not know what an ink blot is, or seems apprehensive about the test, a few words on the making of the blots will be helpful. I myself have found the following instructions useful:

'I am going to show you a series of ink blots. They were made by dropping Indian ink on a piece of paper, and folding it to make some kind of a pattern. I want you to tell me what you can see in them. You may turn the card any way you like; tell me as many things as you can make out, and when you cannot see any more, hand the card back to me.'

With the last words[1] the patient is handed Card I in its standard position, face up, and on the score sheet a note made of the time. An eye is kept on the second-hand in order to be able to make a note of the number of seconds till the first response comes. This may be within a few seconds, or a couple of minutes.

Sometimes a patient will temporize by asking questions about his task, whether he is supposed to look at it as a whole only, whether the white spaces count too, or whether he may pick on some shading in the middle. These are leading questions, and the answer is 'Anything you like'.

There is, in practice, only one thing the patient may not do, and

[1] School children should be warned that there is no 'right' or 'wrong' answer. 'It's just what you see that I want. Anything you see is there, and anyhing you don't see isn't there—so there's no prize and no penalty' (or the like).

24

this is to put the card down and walk away from it to have a look at it from a distance. Such a procedure creates a facile whole-blot response for which no scoring is provided. He should be encouraged to hold the card, if such an instruction is not likely to upset him.

If the instructions have been given clearly and concisely, the patient should require no further help once he is holding the card. Occasionally a person will find the first card uninspiring and after a superficial scrutiny want to hand it back. If it is felt that this is laziness or lack of interest it is permissible to give a little encouragement like 'Why not try again?' Only after two to three minutes should this first rejection be accepted. Any of the subsequent cards can be rejected of course. A normal healthy adult will never do so unless as a deliberate refusal to co-operate.

As each card is taken back, a new one is handed to the patient and the time noted. No further instructions need be given. A casual word, such as : 'And what do you make of this one?' may help to avoid an atmosphere of tension.

Patients inclined to be chatty or distracted should be gently led back to their task. Otherwise no comment should interfere with, or influence the activity of the patient. Where he is started on a train of associations which are leading to some suppressed memory, it may be wise to listen, while deducting the time taken over this interruption from the period for that card.

Frequently doubts will arise as to the exact meaning of a response, of its location, or its motivation. Such responses should be underlined or otherwise marked for inquiry after the sitting. While the test is in progress no question should be asked, because it would convey an element of suggestion which would affect further responses. The only permissible request is one for the part of blot in question to be indicated, and this should only be done on rare occasions.

The length of time taken over each card can be calculated from a note of the actual time of its return.

When Card X has been handed back, the test is over and one can begin to ask questions.

The beginner will find it difficult to decide on the scoring of many responses, and on what might be considered one single response, and what ought to be scored as several. To deal with the second problem first, one picture is called forth by one particular blot or part of a blot, and forms one single response, however much it has been elaborated. It may represent people among objects of scenery, but it is still one uniform response. On the other hand, subsequent inquiry may reveal that, for instance, the 'two men—and a butterfly between them' in Card III do not belong to each other pictorially, but only as separate, unconnected items, and are therefore two separate responses in contrast to 'Two men chasing a butterfly'. More difficult is it to find the correct scoring where the response seems to have been induced by several character traits of the pattern, shape, colour, shading, and sensation of movement. As the spontaneous character of a response is of greater value in the attempt to get an insight into the personality than the more common form-controlled one, it is advisable to score them separately as part of the same response. A response is called 'spontaneous' when it is influenced by more than mere outline of the blot, for instance its colour, shading, or suggestion of movement. A corresponding adjustment made when percentages are calculated, will put matters right again. Rorschach's original idea was that only the predominant character should be scored. But spontaneity is so scarce in certain groups of individuals that a 'red butterfly in flight' must be scored both as a colour and a movement response, unless one wants to risk overlooking some aspect of the patient's personality.

Where doubt exists, the patient is asked to explain after the sitting 'what made him see' the response in question. Leading questions still being avoided, the scoring can then be adjusted.

American Rorschach experts recommend that each patient be 'tested for limits' after the test proper. This method is particularly valuable where no or few spontaneous responses, i.e. those to colour or movement, have been obtained. One wants to discover whether the patient is at all capable of these response types and to what degree. Normally his record should show a number of whole blot responses, of 'popular' ones, of some to movement and to colour. If his record is devoid of some of these, he is shown a card particularly suited for the purpose, the relevant blot pointed out to him, and he is asked what it could be.

To test for the ability to give a 'whole-blot' response Card V is shown, which scores the highest $W$ responses in practice. The patient is asked to look at it again and see whether 'it could also be anything else'.

For movement perception the two figures in Card III are shown, with a similar request. If the patient has identified the human-like figures he may be pressed to say a little more about them. The suggestion of movement is, of course, not permissible, and such questions as 'what are they doing?' must be avoided.

For influence of colour the 'green caterpillars' near the foot of Card X, or the 'pink bow' in the centre of Card III can be used.

For the ability to see the commonplace, the 'animals', the lateral pink blots in Card VIII are the most suitable, as they are identified as such by about 90 per cent of people.

If one feels that there are reasons that the patient should or might give some significant chiaroscuro response, he is shown Card VII for the expected 'cloud' or 'smoke' effect, Card VI for the touch-feeling response frequently evoked by the mottled appearance around the middle, which may be interpreted as wool, fur, cotton, grained wood, or other descriptions of texture. A 'vista response' finally may be evoked by pointing out the spearhead-like little grey blot in Card II in the centre between the upper red blots. People with a gift for perspective will often see in it a 'tree-lined alley ending in steps leading to a temple' or similar picture.

One will soon discover that the expected responses are only made by people who overlooked those items under the pressure of the manifold ideas the respective blots evoked during the test proper. If they are given in the 'testing for limits', they are not scored with the original test responses, but added in brackets as 'additional responses'. The same applies to responses made spontaneously by the patient during the limits test and not in answer to a special request. One usually hears some exclamation like, 'Oh, doctor, there is something I did not see the first time——'. These responses should be taken into consideration, but have not the value of those given during the original test.

Where time is short and the record of satisfactory variety and number of responses, this testing for limits may be omitted.

Only prolonged experience will allow one to evolve the perfect method of approach to the patient. Once such a method has been found, it is essential that it becomes a routine. That is the nearest approach to a standardization of a test which will always preserve a measure of pliability in the hands of the expert. At the same time the very interest of the method lies in comparing the reactions of the various patients to it.

On the whole the response series will be richer both in quality and in quantity if the patient is intelligent and educated. Fifteen to twenty responses of very simple type are usual for a labourer, while a person

27

with secondary school education will average thirty to forty. Sometimes a patient sets out to give as many responses as he can possibly think of, in the mistaken idea that this will give him a high score. He may give sixty to seventy responses to Card I and at the end of two hours he is only starting on Card IV. It is in such cases that it is wise not to deviate from the principle of completing each test in a single sitting, for soon the patient will tire of the game, the responses become fewer per card, and the second half of the card series be dealt with in less time than he took over the first card. Any interruption for meals or rest will only enable the patient to regain strength, to ponder over new methods of interpretation, and to waste valuable time with cheap, superficial responses, whose multitude in no way improve our insight into his personality. If the test has to be interrupted for any reason, it had best be done after Card V, because Card VI re-opens the second half of the series not unlike Card I, and the colour Card VIII and X will once more come as a surprise after VII. But it is always better to finish in a single sitting.

Occasionally a patient will give a bizarre response series, for instance all whole-blot answers, or only anatomical responses. If a patient should have misunderstood the instructions and be under the impression that he must only consider the blot as a whole, he will soon find it such a strain that he will ask a relevant question. The answer 'anything you like' will promptly lead to a wider type of response. But in the vast majority of such freak records they express the patients' inner drive, not his free choice, and are therefore pathognomic.

I once asked a youthful hypochondriac at the end of the sitting why he had given thirty-two consecutive anatomy responses to the ten cards. He replied, plausibly enough, that he had believed them to be medical diagrams. But a re-test a month later showed clearly that he was compelled to think on those lines, for twenty-four of the responses reappeared.

An intelligent and co-operative patient will not be able to resist the interest evoked by the diverse patterns nor the manifold suggestions arising from them. Falsification of the test is a practical impossibility unless the patient be familiar with its mechanism.

A final word about care of the cards. During the years of war they were extremely hard to obtain.

I set out to test a thousand school children, and quickly realized that my set would not survive the first hundred. Although experts deprecate the idea of putting the cards under glass, I ventured to cover them with cellophane, and I have found no alteration in the responses. Very occasionally a child would be distracted by the reflections on the shiny surface, and once a ten-year-old pulled my leg by telling me he could see a boy's face, and laughed gleefully when he saw me write this down, because he knew quite well that his own reflection was not a proper response. If one is always working in the same room it is not difficult to try out a position for the patient where the light will not unduly reflect in the surface of the cards.

The loose edges of the cellophane cover are pasted to the back of the card, and a wet sponge passed over the front. In twenty-four to forty-eight hours the cellophane will present a smooth, even surface that will protect the cards against dirty fingermarks.

Until considerable practice has been gained in 'scoring' the Rorschach Test, the beginner may have difficulty in deciding on the correct symbols to apply to many responses. It is suggested that use be made of the table of contents to this book, which have been made as comprehensive and detailed as possible, so as to form a means of quick reference to the definition, assessment and significance of each scoring symbol and of the more usual types of response.

# 3

## SCORING AND TABULATION

Scoring is not a rigid matter of dogma. Different countries prefer different symbols based on their respective languages, and different experts lay stress on different points of analysis, developing their own scoring system.

I believe it was Guttman who very aptly likened the Rorschach scoring to a 'system of pegs on which to hang one's knowledge of personality'. If the scoring here described follows mainly the scheme of the Rorschach Research Exchange, the choice was directed by its wide scope and the hope that it would enable the beginner to follow the discussions in the majority of modern publications on the subject in the English tongue.

## THE MENTAL APPROACH

By 'mental approach' one understands the manner in which the patient selects parts of the blots for interpretation. The ideal method of approach would be to respond first to the blot as a whole, then to go for major parts of it, and finally to pick out minor details. As this 'approach' to the task, however, shows great and significant individual —as well as group—variations, careful attention must be paid to it. In order to obtain a clear survey of all the facts it is advisable to adopt a methodical system of tabulation, such as is suggested in the diagram. This plan is a slight modification of that put forward by Klopfer and has been found most valuable.

For the beginner, only the basic and essential scoring has been

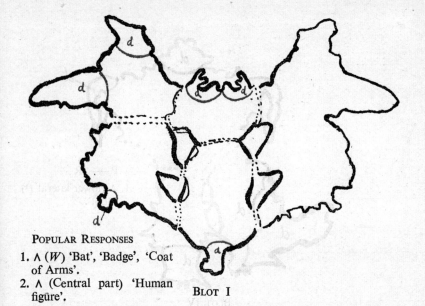

POPULAR RESPONSES

1. ∧ (*W*) 'Bat', 'Badge', 'Coat of Arms'.
2. ∧ (Central part) 'Human figure'.

BLOT I

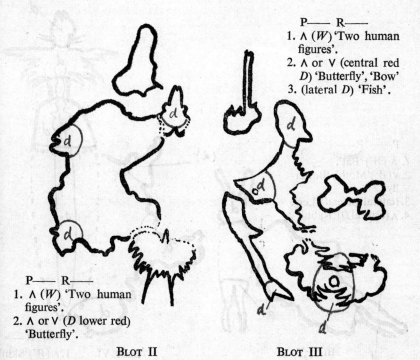

P—— R——
1. ∧ (*W*) 'Two human figures'.
2. ∧ or ∨ (central red *D*) 'Butterfly', 'Bow'
3. (lateral *D*) 'Fish'.

P—— R——
1. ∧ (*W*) 'Two human figures'.
2. ∧ or ∨ (*D* lower red) 'Butterfly'.

BLOT II

BLOT III

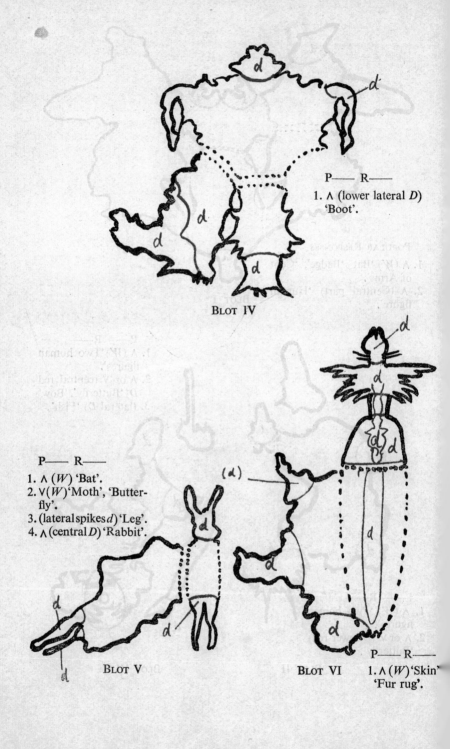

**BLOT IV**

P——— R———
1. ∧ (lower lateral *D*) 'Boot'.

P——— R———
1. ∧ (*W*) 'Bat'.
2. ∨(*W*)'Moth', 'Butter-fly'.
3. (lateral spikes *d*) 'Leg'.
4. ∧ (central *D*) 'Rabbit'.

**BLOT V**

**BLOT VI**

P——— R———
1. ∧ (*W*) 'Skin' 'Fur rug'.

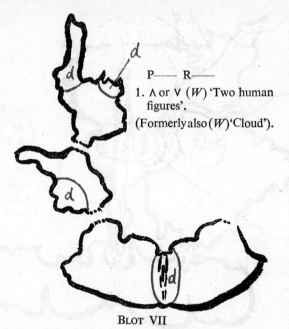

P——— R———

1. Λ or V (*W*) 'Two human figures'.

(Formerly also (*W*)'Cloud').

BLOT VII

P——— R———

1. (lateral red *D*) 'Animal'.

(Formerly also (central ribbed *D*) 'Skeleton').

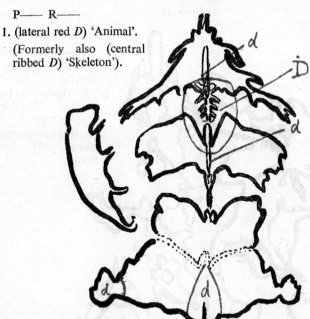

BLOT VIII

C

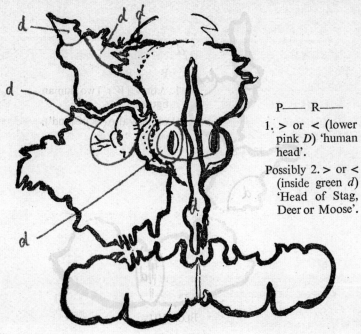

P—— R——

1. > or < (lower pink D) 'human head'.

Possibly 2. > or < (inside green d) 'Head of Stag, Deer or Moose'.

BLOT IX

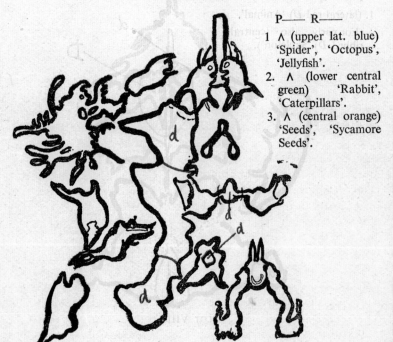

P—— R——

1 ∧ (upper lat. blue) 'Spider', 'Octopus', 'Jellyfish'.

2. ∧ (lower central green) 'Rabbit', 'Caterpillars'.

3. ∧ (central orange) 'Seeds', 'Sycamore Seeds'.

BLOT X

indicated, and a number of lines left blank, where later on more complicated scorings of the rarer type can be inserted. These will be mentioned in the last chapter.

The 'approach' is scored with the help of the tracings showing the divisions of each blot into major and minor details, which have been standardized empirically. In the tracings the parts which are scored as major detail ($D$) are outlined in black, and the line continued by dots where it cuts across the blot. The blot has been taken to pieces like parts of a jig-saw puzzle for clearer illustration. These limits are minimal, that is to say, a major detail of the blot can have neighbouring parts added to it and still be scored as $D$, but should not comprise less than the area mapped out.

Minor detail ($d$) are for our purposes the most frequently chosen small parts, and are therefore specially mapped out in red. Less commonly selected detail of the same size or smaller is not mapped out because it is collectively classified under $dd$.

1. '$W$' stands for 'whole', and is applicable wherever all parts of the blot have entered into one single response. The response may be a single figure or object, or an elaborate scene.

2. '☆' is used only in Cards II and III, and signifies that the response was given to the black parts of the blot only, while the red was ignored. It is neither a $W$ nor a $D$ response, and is therefore scored differently.

3. The '$D$' stands for 'major detail', and may consist of anything from almost the whole blot to those divisions outlined in the diagrams. Roughly speaking, any part of the blot that covers about a quarter of the whole is a $D$; also those parts which are separated from the parent blot by a dividing edge of white ground or are of a separate colour. Thus each of the three red blots in Cards II and III are $D$, and in the coloured Cards VIII, IX and X each individual colour separates it from the others and makes of itself a major detail.

In Card X the individually coloured blots are very small, but they are also completely detached or nearly so, and therefore attract attention with the same power as, for instance, the much bigger 'boot' in Card IV. In Card X the main parts of the upper central grey ('gargoyles' and 'post') and of the lower central green ('rabbit's head' and 'caterpillars') are also scored '$D$'. Neither the $D$, nor the $W$ and ☆ scores are affected by the deliberate exclusion of some minor detail for purposes of closer similarity with the response content.

4. The '$d$' is the *common* minor detail. These have been carefully

standardized and are important. In the diagram they have been mapped out by a red line separating them from the parent blot. This line is not to be taken as the accurate delineation of that detail, but as an indication of its position and approximate size. Frequently only the outline is used for the response and the deeper parts ignored: this is still a '*d*' response. On the other hand, a patient may go out from such a minor detail and incorporate considerably more of the rest than the red line indicates: if the size is less than *D* it is still a '*d*' response.

5. The '*dd*' refers to all parts of the blot which are neither *D* nor *d*, varying in size from 'too small for *D*' to that of the smallest *d*, such as the 'tree' or 'wheat sheaf' along the outer lower edge of Card I. This allows us to incorporate Rorschach's 'rare responses' in the scoring system in an easier way. They should still be well recognizable, and be identifiable without any effort. They should therefore not be smaller than the head of a matchstick. Parts of any blot in Card X are *dd*, unless very minute, or as indicated on the tracing.

6. The '*ddd*' is reserved for minute detail. This is clinically not the same as the last, as experience with children and some other groups of the population show. These minute details are usually small spikes or knobs along the edge of the blot, but they may also be picked out of the shading in the centre or be completely detached from the blot like the dots around the base of Blot I.

While the previously mentioned small detail had still a distinguishable shape, the '*ddd*' group are merely pegs on which to hang the products of imagination. Children in a certain stage of mental development, for instance, will frequently respond to a tiny spike not larger than a pin's head along the edge of a blot with an elaborate description of a moving person, when even a magnifying glass will fail to disclose any real similarity.

7. '*S*' stands for 'space' and refers to all white spaces. These may be large or small, isolated or combined with part of the blot. An analysis of a large series of these responses has failed to reveal any essential significance attaching to these variations in size or combination. They are not frequent and when met they are seldom numerous. The important factor is that the pattern has been reversed and the empty spaces chosen for interpretation. Where these space responses are mainly small details, the tendency for selection of small or minute detail will show itself so clearly in the tabulation of *dd* and *ddd*, that this character can be ignored in the *S*. Combina-

tions of space and blot, on the other hand, have some significance (Beck's *Organizing Talent*, *Z*) of which more will be said in the last chapter.

Here it seems advisable to score all white space responses under the single symbol '*S*'. The central light area in Blot IX may be scored as *S* or as *D*, according to whether it is contrasted with its surroundings, or conceived as part of them.

## PERSONALITY STRUCTURE

The structure of the basic personality is outlined by the proportion in which certain scores appear in the final summary. These scores relate to the mental process which has translated the shape or colour of the blot into a picture. This is the most difficult part of the test for the operator, and it is wise to start from simple principles and gradually to elaborate as experience shows the need for it.

As has been indicated previously, the response may be a mere mechanical interpretation of outline as a picture of some object. Or the blot may stimulate a process of phantasy to perceive movement, or its colour may dictate the response. For each of these processes there are qualitative degrees, though the criteria are not the same. Pure form is classified as average, exceptionally good or well seen, and exceptionally poor. The colour responses are graded according to the degree of form perception which has entered into them. The movement responses are all based on form perception to start with. While colour without form is possible, movement without form is so rare that its incidence can be disregarded by the beginner. The variations of movement type are evolutionally and clinically determined; human movement coincides with the maturing of human phantasy and is rare before the age of eight years, up to which age moving animals are the common expression. Inanimate movement, such as swaying trees, spraying fountains, explosions, are linked with clinical pictures, and are therefore again a class apart.

The variations in the chiaroscuro responses to shadings of tones of grey are determined by the influence of form on the picture seen, and the same applies to the touch-feeling response, and the 'black or white as colour' response.

It seems convenient to define the scoring of these responses in the order of their appearance on the tabulation sheet, irrespective of predominance or significance in the personality structure as a whole.

## MOVEMENT RESPONSES

1. '*m*' is evolutionally and clinically the lowest form of movement response. It is scored where the moving object is neither animal nor human. An exception is made for small parts of the human body seen as separate entities and suggesting a certain amount of movement, such as 'staring eyes', 'pointing fingers', 'clutching hands'. The main bulk of '*m*' response consists of objects swaying, falling, hanging, rising, water rushing, running, spouting, clouds drifting, fire flickering, 'volcanoes erupting', 'guns flashing', 'charges exploding', 'blood spurting'. It will be seen from this that form perception here is frequently at a low level, and that many responses are derived from the chiaroscuro or from colour. The response is therefore most frequently scored as a combination with either $K$ or $C$. As chiaroscuro is tabulated next to movement, it is not difficult to fit such a combined $m$ and $K$ into the scheme without upsetting the balance of the whole picture. If it is considered that movement sensation is the predominant factor in the response, and the shading only secondary, it is scored as $mK$. But for the majority of such combinations the chiaroscuro is the primary, and the movement the secondary thought. The interpretation of a blot as water, cloud, or fire (if grey) is suggested by the shades of grey and an element of form, and their movement added to them. This $Km$ is conveniently tabulated on the line above $K$.

More difficult is it to assess the scoring for combinations of colour and such movement—for instance, spurting blood. As these scores are tabulated on different sides of the balance held by $F$ the decision is of some importance, particularly as the response is of clinical significance and not rare. My personal impression is that the colour score is the more important, and that for the vast majority of such responses the appropriate scoring is $Cm$, and its proper place between $CF$ and $C$, if there is a good form element contained in it (like 'a tree swaying in the breeze') or after $C$ if it is not (like 'running blood'). This applies obviously only to Cards II, III, VIII, IX and X.

Another practice is to score $m$ separately and $K$ or $C$ separately, and make the necessary adjustment for the calculation of percentages afterwards. I would suggest this method to beginners until they have gained enough experience in the incidence and significance of $K$ and of $C$ to start working on the combinations with '*m*'.

2. '*FM*' refers to moving animals, from the 'hanging bat' to the

'galloping horse' and the 'fighting bear'. The symbol is unfortunate. as '*AM*' would be more appropriate. But it seems to have been universally accepted, and must therefore be continued if the existing literature is not going to be complicated yet more. It arose from the supposition that it represented a more form-controlled response than the human movement, *M*. Thus an *F* was placed before the *M* in the way of the colour scores. There should be little difficulty about this response.

3. '*M*' is the symbol for human movement. The beginner will find it more convenient to group under it all human figures described as doing something, from the 'standing man' and the 'sleeping beauty' to the 'boxing negroes'. Rorschach barred animal movements extended to human figures, such as 'angels flying'; the basic response, however, is the human form, and any of its activities, whether fictitious or practical, should score *M*.

Further variations of *M* will be discussed in the final chapter. They are not essential at this stage.

## CHIAROSCURO RESPONSES

1. '*K*' is pure chiaroscuro, a grey-in-grey of vague outline or shape, such as water, cloud, smoke. To this group also belongs 'darkness', the sense of 'dreariness' or 'threatening' derived from the shading, not so much in the sense of colour as of a vague, abstract or nightlike quality. The essential character of this response is its shapelessness, its misty, fluid quality, or its depressing, displeasing tone. The patient reacts to the mottled shades of grey, and the outline of the blot is ignored or its significance minimized.

2. '*k*' is more form-controlled than *K*. It is used for a large variety of responses derived from the shading. X-ray pictures, and photographs, relief maps, all faces, heads, or figures of humans or animals, microscopic enlargements of insects, cells, or other objects, picked out of the mottling inside any blot and independent of its edge.

3. '*FK*' is the most form-controlled of the chiaroscuro responses. It is used for perspective, the 'vista' response in which shades of grey, possibly with the addition of white spaces, are interpreted as alleys leading to a house, mountain ranges going into the distance, people hiding behind bushes, cottages obscured by trees in front of them, any response which clearly expresses a perception of distance and perspective based on the shading.

Some responses are difficult to classify, such as 'rocks' where the element of chiaroscuro is not easily assessed, or caves[1] through which one looks into light, white spaces as light or water by contrast with the grey which is interpreted as earth or stone. The clinical significance of such responses is as yet not established to the best of my knowledge, and while I often feel inclined to regard some of them as a form of $K$, I would suggest that for the time being they be scored as $F$, $F+$, or $F-$, according to their quality. Particular judgment is necessary where the response suggests a reflected image in water; this is often based more on an appreciation of symmetry than of qualities of the chiaroscuro.

## PURE FORM RESPONSES

1. $F$ stands for the pure form of the blot determining the response. While Rorschach divided all $F$ responses into $+$ and $-$, some experts prefer to reserve these qualitative symbols for those more exceptional instances where form is either outstandingly good or where it is very badly seen. Such objects as 'a torn and tattered leaf', 'seaweed', or 'a stone' can obviously fit almost any shape of blot and are therefore not responses resulting from a careful examination of the blot, but from a careless comparison. Less frequently one comes across a response picture of definite shape but totally unsuited to the blot under consideration. This happens almost exclusively in cases of perseveration of ideas, where, for instance, a patient has defined the shape of a tree in one card and continues identifying every subsequent blot with a tree. Such responses are $F-$, as should also be classed the frequent 'rocks', and the vague 'maps' which do not refer to any particular part of the globe.

2. $F+$ are responses where form has been closely identified in the blot, such as faces bearing resemblance to a known personality, or figures and objects described to some detail. It has been suggested that any response with a qualifying adjective should be ranged among the $F+$. Experience with children and with very different types of adults has shown that such mechanical standardization would lead to gross misinterpretations. Some patients are inclined to respond in sentences, others in monosyllables or nearly so. From both groups good, bad, and average responses may be obtained, and the voluble talker would obtain too high a score, while the taciturn person would score too low. The responses must therefore

[1] See p. 127.

be sifted and judged according to merit. Thus, for example, the response 'flying fox' to Card V is superior to 'a bat with wings and a head': in the former case an attempt at accuracy has been made by taking specific forms into consideration, while in the latter the elaborating detail is pointless, since all bats have wings and a head.

The majority of responses will be 'average form', *F*. After working with the test for a little while one becomes familiar with the average quality of form response and can differentiate between the three degrees without much difficulty.

## THE SURFACE TEXTURE RESPONSES

'Small *c*' has been chosen as the symbol for surface texture or 'touch-feeling' responses. Such a response is based on an interpretation of the shading as texture, for instance wool, hair, cloth, stone. Or elaboration of the surface as for instance in carvings or mouldings. Such responses arise from the experience of touch, as if passing one's fingers over an object.

There is also another type of response, which though allied to it, is not formed on 'touch-feeling': this is the interpretation of the shading as surface pattern, for instance the grain of wood, or the pattern of chintz. Here the surface is conceived as flat, and although it has still the quality of texture, the response was inspired by utilizing the shades of grey as if they were tones of colour.

It is this last consideration that has induced Klopfer[1] to range this 'small *c*' on that side of *F* where the extratensive responses are scored. The touch-feeling response proper, as described in the first paragraph, could have been classified among the chiaroscuro responses, and the pioneer Binder still does so. But the significance of the response places it in a class by itself. The *K* responses are a phantasy process, a reaction of conscious and unconscious discomfort to the grey and black, rationalized in the *k* and *FK* responses by the censorship of form imposed on it. Touch-feeling is a different mental process. This type of response is frequently linked with 'surface pattern', or merges into the latter almost imperceptibly. It appears therefore justifiable to group these two 'small *c*' responses on the outwardly emotional side of *F* as practised by Klopfer.

Pure *c* responses are not very common. Usually there is a pronounced element of form in them, like the 'thick lion skin with the darker hair along the back and the bushy tail' for Card VI, or the

[1] See *Rorschach Research Exchange, 1938–40.*

'finely grained walnut cabinet' for Card IV. Such responses are *Fc*. Where it is clear that texture was the primary stimulus and form, possibly less appropriate, an additional thought, the scoring is *cF*.

## THE PSEUDO COLOUR RESPONSES, BLACK, GREY, WHITE

*C'* is the symbol for responses which have interpreted black, white, or grey as a colour. In 'small *c*' these shades were used as tones and patterns, and such a response as 'grained walnut or mahogany' is obviously not based on an identity with colour. In the *K* group of responses black or grey was interpreted as 'darkness' or 'haziness'. As *C'* are scored such responses as 'a man in black' for Card VI, 'a blackbird' for Card V, 'a grey squirrel' for Card VI, or 'snow' for a white space.

As in the previous group of scores, so here the combination with the form factor determines whether a response is *FC'*, *C'F*, or *C'*.

## THE COLOUR RESPONSES

*FC*, *CF*, and *C* are the symbols for the real colour responses to Cards II, III, VIII, IX, and X. With a little practice and experience it will not be found very difficult to arrive at the appropriate score for each response.

A pure *C* response is devoid of all form. Such responses are 'blood', 'sky', 'paint', 'a green field', 'earth', 'sand', and similar generalizations. 'Water', where it is based purely on a similarity of colour and not on the finer shadings, should also be scored in this way.

The differentiation between *FC* and *CF* depends on the degree of form consideration given to the response. This requires practice, but is not really difficult. If the central red in Card III is called a 'red butterfly' or a 'red bow' it is obvious that form determined the response in the first place and the colour similarity was expressed as an after-thought. In Card VIII the pink 'animal' at the side is often identified with a 'chameleon'. It is very difficult to specify the 'animal', and the chameleon is about the only one which might show such an unusual colour, whilst harmonizing pretty well with the shape of the blot. Such responses are scored as *FC*. Whether the not infrequently given response of 'fox' to that same blot should be scored as *FC* should be decided by subsequent inquiry in each individual case.

A *CF* response is one in which the colour of the blot has stimulated the choice of answer, and the similarity in shape is vague, inappropriate, or merely possible. Such a score would be given to 'a tree' to the green blot in Card IX, or to 'a flower' response to the orange and pink in the lower part of Card VIII. The 'red cloud' sometimes given to the lower lateral red-brown in Card X or similar blots could also be so scored, although the cloud effect is chiaroscuro. My own experience is that a patient susceptible to chiaroscuro will give $K$ responses to the grey cards before doing so to the coloured ones. Where he has not given a $K$ response before, it must be assumed that he has succumbed to the influence of colour, and his 'red cloud', 'brown smoke' or similar answer belongs to the $CF$ or even $C$ score.[1]

The responses tabulated here are the basic requirement for the beginner. They are sufficient for all main practical purposes where one is not searching for finer nuances of the personality. Responses which cannot be fitted with confidence into any of the score groups outside $F$, should be scored, either $F$, $F+$, or $F-$. The end result will not be materially affected. It is a greater mistake to enlarge either the movement—or the colour score with responses that do not belong to those groups at all, than to score them as form. Where reasonable doubts exist one should have recourse to Rorschach's method of making a note of certain trends which seemed indicated but which were not clearly expressed in words. Such 'trends to movement responses' or 'trends to colour responses' are a valuable hint to the latent personality, and may appear in a scoreable form at a subsequent re-test.

## THE CONTENT

By 'Content' is meant the essential picture which the blot has stimulated in the patient's mind, viz., the main feature of the response. This content is classified in various groups. For the scoring, this grouping is more important than the individual character of the response which will come under full consideration at a later stage in the interpretation of the test record. There are several points to which attention must be paid, and a clear and comprehensive tabulation will help to remind the beginner of them.

### ANIMAL RESPONSES, *A*

The response most frequently obtained is the animal response. Its incidence has a bearing on the clinical picture, and as it is the one

[1] See p. 128.

to which Rorschach paid greatest attention, it has been placed at the head of the list. A distinction is made between the 'whole animal' response, *A*, and where only an incomplete animal is seen, *Ad*. Such animal detail may be no more than a 'donkey's ears', or 'a hoof', or it may be the rump complete with head.

## HUMAN FIGURE RESPONSES, *H*

The human figure response, *H*, or, if seen as a part only, *Hd* (human detail) comes about next in frequency. These two responses, animal and human, are not only nearly always present, but they are always important, be it in health or disease. Objects of animal origin like eggs, skins, shells, are conveniently grouped under the heading of 'Animal Objects', *A/Obj.*, and garments—hats, shoes, coats, etc.— under 'Human Objects', *H/Obj*.

## ORDINARY RESPONSES

The remaining responses can roughly be grouped into those which are common and ordinary, but without particular pathognomic significance in themselves other than to indicate variety of content, and those which are not frequently met apart from abnormal conditions of the personality.

The common response groups into which practically all the ordinary intimate responses can be placed, are architecture, geography, landscape, object, and vegetable, to quote them in alphabetical order.

## PATHOGNOMIC RESPONSES

The most important and the most frequent pathognomic responses are anatomy, blood, cloud, and fire.

There are others about whose significance one cannot dogmatize so readily. Some clearly belong to the last group—for instance sexual details, flesh, smoke, X-ray pictures, explosions. Others strike one as too unusual to be listed among the ordinary responses, and it is a good practice to tabulate them under their own heading, if for no better reason than to draw attention to them. Thus one may obtain an overwhelming number of 'rocks', 'stones', or 'cliffs', to which little importance would be attached if these items occurred as isolated instances, but which assume significance by their repetition. 'Water' is usually a *K* response, and where it forms part of an elaborated picture, its basis should be investigated, and if found to be due to chiaroscuro, scored as such. Where 'water' occurs repeatedly, or where it is given a special character or movement, it should be tabulated, whereas when only a part of a geographical description, it may be no more than a second thought.

Children of an early school age frequently content themselves with 'form-description' (*F-descr.*) instead of true interpretation. They describe squares, circles, triangles, or lines.

In other groups of individuals, for instance, those suffering from organic brain lesions, mere colour naming replaces the usual response to colour (*Cn*). This must not be confounded with the more commonly met with comment on colour or exclamation provoked by colour.

Another form of response is the interpretation of the blot as an abstract idea (*Abstr.*). For instance: 'There is an atmosphere of peace about this (blot)', or: 'I get the impression of tremendous effort, of powers being at work.'

Such tendencies should be tabulated when they occur. It is therefore a good practice to have a few blank lines among or at the end of the list of contents where such items can be inserted.

# QUANTITY AND QUALITY OF THE RESPONSES

## DISTRIBUTION OF RESPONSES, *R*

Under this heading are tabulated the number of responses, *R*, per card.

## THE POPULAR RESPONSES, *P*

*P*, the number of 'popular' responses per card. These *P* responses have been empirically tabulated for each card, and will be found on the diagrams of the blots. They are the responses most commonly given to certain blots or parts of them.

## THE ORIGINAL RESPONSE, *O*

*O*, is the scoring symbol for 'original', and is given to a response whose content has that character. It has been defined as a response which is derived from the personal and unusual experience of the patient. It is most frequently a specific, uncommon object; but it may be abstract, scientific, personal, or take any other form.

*O* is also scored where several parts of the blot are used in a very original combination to furnish a good response. Such a response should not recur more often than once in a hundred patients of that particular group of personality to which that patient belongs.

## THE AVERAGE TIME

Time average for each response. This is most conveniently noted as number of minutes for each card divided by the number of responses for it. The latter item is found under *R*.

## THE TIME FOR THE FIRST RESPONSE

Time for the first response to each card does not require further explanation.

## THE ADDITIONAL RESPONSES

Additional Responses. Here a survey is taken of all additional responses which occurred during or after the sitting, as while testing for 'limits' or while inquiring into doubtful responses. The actual scoring of these additional responses is tabulated in brackets in their appropriate places. Here merely their number is recorded.

# THE CHARACTER OF THE RESPONSE

To remind the beginner of the many points to which he has to give his attention in this test, it will be found useful to make a list of the most common types, and to score them if found. In the last chapter some of the rarer characters of the response will be mentioned on account of their significance in certain clinical pictures.

## 'CONFABULATION'

This is the tendency to see in some part of a blot far more than its most accurate scrutiny justifies. For instance a small detail may be described as 'a boy with a cudgel going over a hill to a castle where he is going to slay the king of the giants'. The actual blot seen suggests the 'boy with the cudgel'—and possibly a hill. The rest is imagination or confabulation.

## MORBID RESPONSES

These have recently received special attention during the years of war. Such a score is given to 'squashed beetles', 'bleeding' or 'headless' animals or human figures, diseased or disfigured creatures, responses expressing suffering or death.

## THE 'SCHIZOID' RESPONSE

This type of response is based on the theory that the schizoid personality has a tendency to live in two worlds at the same time, and that his phantasy content reflects this process. The responses express an atmosphere of unreality, e.g. human figures with two heads or otherwise deformed, or wearing feathers; monsters, pre-historic animals, devils, combinations of man and animal, animated trees and other vegetables, fairies and fairy-tale landscapes, scenes from Mars. An exception are references to well-known works of art or illustrations of such fiction as Peter Pan, Alice in Wonderland, or Walt Disney's characters.

## REMARKS

Remarks should be relevant for purpose of scoring, such as comments on shape, tone, or colour of the blot, expressions of like or dislike of a card, or criticisms of or enthusiasm for the task.

## EXCLAMATIONS

These are a more explosive form of remark, from a simple 'oh' or 'hush' or a whistle, to the more elaborate expression of feelings involving expletives.

## QUESTION-FORM OF RESPONSE

Many people—particularly children—will turn the response into a question: 'Could this be a bat?' 'Is it a man?'

## SEXUAL RESPONSES

These are usually contained in anatomical or human responses. Any stress of sex characteristics in the anatomical sense, particularly when referring to sex organs, should be noted, and scored here as a peculiar character of the responses listed among the content.[1]

## REJECTIONS

The rejection of a card is a gross abnormality of response to the task. Such a rejection must be accepted when the patient has made a definite effort at interpretation and is unable to do so after several

[1] See note, p. 88.

minutes. The average time a patient studies the card before he decides that he can make nothing of it, is three to five minutes. Only when dealing with Card I is it permissible to encourage the patient with a 'try again!' if he is trying to hand the card back in less than three minutes. Sometimes a patient is mentally lazy and wants to escape the task at the start; such behaviour can often be aborted by a mild insistence. Otherwise the final test result may present a misleading picture. A deliberate refusal to co-operate has not the value of a 'rejection', for it expresses antagonism to the test principle or to the person of the tester instead of to the blot and its character. A genuine rejection arises from the patient's inability to make anything of the blot, and presumes the patient's sincere effort to discover something. Only where the sight of a blot causes obvious distress to the patient should a rejection be accepted within a shorter space of time.

The patient's mere assurance that he 'cannot see anything' is not a rejection until he complies with the instructions he has received and hands the card back. Many patients grumble about the task and talk of giving it up, while continuing to scrutinize and turn the card. As long as they continue to do so one should ignore this behaviour, though noting it. A lift of the head or a movement of the hands may be taken as a sign of agreement by the patient and induce him to follow his words with the action of actually handing the card back. Not infrequently, such grumblers persevere and finally produce a response after five or more minutes.

## TURNING

The way in which patients handle the cards varies considerably. Some will turn it in various directions in rapid succession before and between responses, giving each position no more than a cursory glance before hurrying on to a new one as if hoping that inspiration may come from this procedure. Others, finding the standard position stimulating, will not turn again until they have exhausted all the possibilities, and thus proceed methodically in the four main positions. Still others will not turn the card at all and content themselves with responding to it in the same position. There are also individuals who turn the card upside down the moment they receive it and insist on giving their first responses to it in this position.

Turning is called 'optimal' when it best serves the purpose of the test. This purpose demands that the blot be looked at from all directions, particularly the four main ones. Where method enters into the patients' approach to the test, one may find that some will exhaust the response possibilities of one position before going to the next, while others will try to find first all the *W*, then *D*, then *d*, and finally *dd+S* responses, turning the card afresh for each purpose. For either of these groups of individuals turning will be optimal, though the actual number of turns will differ considerably. The actual amount of turning is less significant than the purpose it serves.

Turning may be 'excessive', when it exceeds the requirements of normal, rational purpose. A moderate number of abortive turns always occurs in an optimal procedure, but this should not become a haphazard turning around of the card.

Finally, turning may be 'inadequate' when the patient fails to look at the card from at least three different positions.

He may reason within himself that the blots are symmetrical, and that therefore one lateral view is like the other. His three main positions must therefore be at least upright, upside down, and lateral view to be 'minimal optimal'. Anything less is 'inadequate'.

Between these main headings—'optimal', 'excessive' and 'inadequate'—variations can be created at discretion. We have already mentioned the 'minimal optimal'; another useful term is 'haphazard' or 'pointless', if the patient for instance turns and re-turns repeatedly in two directions, giving the third alternative only a cursory glance.

## THE LAST THREE CARDS

This score refers to the total number of responses given to the last three cards—Card VIII, IX and X. My personal practice is to insert this in the line above the tabulation of the number of responses per card, but it could equally well be fitted below. A test record with many varieties of response will often fill up every available line of the tabulation sheet when many details are noted. The position given to the 'last three cards' score is therefore an attempt at economy of space.

## THE TABULATION OF PERCENTAGE

The figures for the various scores are entered in their respective spaces, and their total number put into the first right-hand column, headed 'Total'. In the adjoining column goes the percentage for each score.

# Scoring and Tabulation

The percentage is calculated by multiplying the individual score total by 100 and dividing by the total number of responses.[1] Where several scores have been entered for one single response these excess scores are added to the total of responses before assessing the percentage.[2]

It is convenient to make a note of the total number of responses and of the total time taken for them at the head of the sheet. The average proportion is one response per minute, and a gross deviation from this can be seen at a glance.

[1] For example: Total responses: 25; $K$ responses: 3;

$$K = \frac{3 \times 100}{25} = 12\%$$

[2] For example: Total responses: 48. But two responses contained elements of both $K$ and $m$ which were scored separately.

$$\text{Total score for } K \text{ was 5;} \quad K = \frac{5 \times 100}{50} = 10\%$$

$$\text{Total score for } m \text{ was 4;} \quad m = \frac{4 \times 100}{50} = 8\%$$

For $F+$ and $F-$ the respective percentage is based on the total $F$, i.e. $(F+ (F+)+(F-))$, not on the total of responses. To arrive at the $F+$ per cent, its total is multiplied by 100 and divided by $(F+(F+)+(F-))$ and the same is done for $F-$.

For example: Total responses: 62; $(18F + 8(F+) + 2(F-)) = 28$;

$$\text{Total } F = \frac{28 \times 100}{62} = 45\%$$

$$\text{But } F+ = \frac{8 \times 100}{28} = 28 \cdot 6\%, \quad \text{and } F- = \frac{2 \times 100}{28} = 7\%$$

| Mental Approach | TABULATION | | | | | | | | | | Total | Per cent |
|---|---|---|---|---|---|---|---|---|---|---|---|---|
| | Total Responses: Total Time: | | | | | | | | | | | |
| Scoring | I | II | III | IV | V | VI | VII | VIII | IX | X | | |
| W | | | | | | | | | | | | |
| | | | | | | | | | | | | |
| W̶ | | | | | | | | | | | | |
| | | | | | | | | | | | | |
| D | | | | | | | | | | | | |
| d | | | | | | | | | | | | |
| dd | | | | | | | | | | | | |
| ddd | | | | | | | | | | | | |
| | | | | | | | | | | | | |
| S | | | | | | | | | | | | |
| | | | | | | | | | | | | |
| | | | | | | | | | | | | |
| | | | | | | | | | | | | |
| | | | | | | | | | | | | |
| | | | | | | | | | | | | |
| | | | | | | | | | | | | |

NOTE—For practical purposes it will be found convenient to lay out 'Mental Approach' and 'Personality Structure' on one sheet, and 'Content', 'Quantity', and 'Quality', 'Last 3 Cards', and 'Character of Response' on another.

| Personality Structure | Total Responses: Total Time: | | | | | | | | | | Total | Per cent |
|---|---|---|---|---|---|---|---|---|---|---|---|---|
| *Scoring* | I | II | III | IV | V | VI | VII | VIII | IX | X | | |
| *m* | | | | | | | | | | | | |
| *FM* | | | | | | | | | | | | |
| *M* | | | | | | | | | | | | |
| *K* | | | | | | | | | | | | |
| *k* | | | | | | | | | | | | |
| *FK* | | | | | | | | | | | | |
| *F* | | | | | | | | | | | | |
| *F+* | | | | | | | | | | | | |
| *F−* | | | | | | | | | | | | |
| *Fc* | | | | | | | | | | | | |
| *FC'* | | | | | | | | | | | | |
| *FC* | | | | | | | | | | | | |
| *CF* | | | | | | | | | | | | |
| *C* | | | | | | | | | | | | |

| Content Scoring | I | II | III | IV | V | VI | VII | VIII | IX | X | Total | Per cent |
|---|---|---|---|---|---|---|---|---|---|---|---|---|
| A | | | | | | | | | | | | |
| Ad | | | | | | | | | | | | |
| | | | | | | | | | | | | |
| H | | | | | | | | | | | | |
| Hd | | | | | | | | | | | | |
| | | | | | | | | | | | | |
| Arch. | | | | | | | | | | | | |
| Geog. | | | | | | | | | | | | |
| Landsc. | | | | | | | | | | | | |
| Object | | | | | | | | | | | | |
| Veget. | | | | | | | | | | | | |
| | | | | | | | | | | | | |
| Anat. | | | | | | | | | | | | |
| Blood | | | | | | | | | | | | |
| Cloud | | | | | | | | | | | | |
| Fire | | | | | | | | | | | | |
| | | | | | | | | | | | | |
| | | | | | | | | | | | | |
| | | | | | | | | | | | | |

| Qual.+ Quant. | | | | | | | | | | | Total | Per cent |
|---|---|---|---|---|---|---|---|---|---|---|---|---|
| Scoring | I | II | III | IV | V | VI | VII | VIII | IX | X | | |
| R | | | | | | | | | | | | |
| Last three cards | | | | | | | | | | →| | |
| P | | | | | | | | | | | | |
| O | | | | | | | | | | | | |
| Time Average | | | | | | | | | | | | |
| Time 1st. R. | | | | | | | | | | | | |
| Addit. Rs. | | | | | | | | | | | | |

54

| Character of R. | | | | | | | | | | | Total | Per cent |
|---|---|---|---|---|---|---|---|---|---|---|---|---|
| *Scoring* | I | II | III | IV | V | VI | VII | VIII | IX | X | | |
| Confab. | | | | | | | | | | | | |
| Morbid | | | | | | | | | | | | |
| Schizoid | | | | | | | | | | | | |
| Remarks | | | • | | | | | | | | | |
| Exclam. | | | | | | | | | | | | |
| Question-form | | | | | | | | | | | | |
| Sexual | | | | | | | | | | | | |
| Rejection | | | | | | | | | | | | |
| | | | | | | | | | | | | |
| | | | | | | | | | | | | |
| Turning | | | | | | | | | | | | |

# 4

## THE SIGNIFICANCE OF THE SEPARATE SCORES

In order to lead to a comprehensive understanding of the test it seems best to try first to explain the significance of each of the scores collected and tabulated, and to discuss later their assessment for the purpose of personality construction from their relative incidence. It is not the single, isolated item of the scoring that is significant, but its appearance within the framework of the total. Many responses may be normal in one personality picture, and abnormal in another. To interpret a test record by picking out a few outstanding features while ignoring the rest can only lead to gross errors in diagnosis.

While we are therefore here attempting to analyse the meaning of the various responses and their scores one by one, it must be clearly understood that it is for the purpose of discussing basic principles only.

### THE MENTAL APPROACH

Under 'Mental Approach' one understands the manner in which the patient approaches the blot for the purpose of finding in it similarities to his world of reality or phantasy, which will produce in his mind a picture, the response. His choice of the whole blot or its details for this purpose is by no means haphazard, but founded on basic tendencies in his character.

### THE *W* RESPONSE

To have 'an eye for the thing as a whole' is common in the young child who has not yet developed the gift of observation of details. Many people in the humbler walks of life never rise above this level. For the *W* response has the significance of a mental fixation at a childhood level; it is the expression of a simplicity of mental outlook which those who have delved deeper into the problems of existence have lost in the course of years. There is a stage of development in the child, when school and personal experience has taught it the value of observation of detail; at this stage, the pendulum swings to the other extreme—a process so characteristic of the years of childhood—and *W* responses become scarce. One might say that the child's life now consists of detailed training which leaves little room for contemplation of existence as a whole. Then comes adolescence, and the entry into the world of the adult; youthful ambition tackles fearlessly the most momentous problems of life, pleasing itself in abstracts and finalities, heedless of arguments and obstacles. Once more we find a predilection for *W* responses in this group of human beings, not as an expression of simplification of the problem, but as a trend to abstract ideas and ideals.

In the intelligent adult the *W* response is therefore interpreted as a tendency towards major issues or abstract ideas. They can be inadequate in number and quality, or excessive, while in a person of low intelligence they are a sign of mental simplicity.

## THE ⅏ RESPONSE

This is an attempt on the part of the patient to produce a whole blot response, but he has found himself unable to include the coloured patches. It is a '*W* failure', due to the disturbing influence of a single bright colour. The significance of the ⅏ response is that of a certain amount of emotional lability. But here again it should not be assessed in this light by itself, for only within the framework of the other responses can it be given this value. Where, for instance, a patient is unable to give a *W* response to Cards I, IV, and V, one is obviously dealing with an inaptitude to 'see the problem as a whole', and the ⅏ responses to Cards II and III merely emphasize this weakness.

The response is more than a major detail answer, for these two blots, Cards II and III, are frequently divided into symmetrical halves of which only one is selected for interpretation, which then constitutes a *D* response. I would suggest that the ⅏ responses be given half a *W* value in the sum of all whole blot responses, for instance:

W responses     Total    4

W̶ responses     „     2

Total $(W + W̶) =$   5

This final sum does not appear in the tabulation, but, like the sum of $(FC+CF+C)$, only in the subsequent scheme for the interpretation of the total test result.

## THE MAJOR DETAIL RESPONSE, *D*

The mental attitude which induces a patient who has either exhausted the possibilities of the whole blot, or failed to be stimulated by it, to select a major detail next, is one of common sense. In the Rorschach blots many major details bear a striking likeness to familiar objects—animate or inanimate. They are therefore the least difficult to interpret, and the patient's common sense dictates that they be given preference.

*D* therefore symbolizes the *common sense factor*.

These, like all other responses, should appear in a definite ratio to other types in the Mental approach. While an insufficient number usually points to a lack of common sense, the mere opposite cannot be said when they are in excess. There is no 'excess of common sense', for the term implies an optimal function. The interpretation of such disproportions will be discussed in the next chapter.

## THE SMALL DETAIL RESPONSE, *d*

By itself it does not appear to have any constant or important psychological significance. It should appear in the proper proportion to the *W* and *D* responses, and its interpretation be based on this ratio. The *d* response arises from the patient's capacity for paying attention to such details, which by their shape or position are almost as conspicuous as the major detail, and from which they differ mainly in their smaller size. It is, however, not so much common sense as attention to the task which drives the patient to their selection. Their clinical significance becomes apparent where they are deficient or excessive in number at the cost of one or more of the other scores. The psychological deduction is logical.

## THE SMALLER, UNUSUAL DETAIL RESPONSE, *dd*, AND THE MINUTE DETAIL RESPONSE, *ddd*

These two responses are conveniently discussed together, as they usually affect the personality picture in conjunction with each other as 'unusual responses'. The patient's mental attitude in these selections may be one of ambition to show his perspicacity, it may be one of avoiding the common paths of life for the unusual and unorthodox, or a tendency to be attracted by the petty side-issues of a problem rather than by what is important. It may symbolize an escape from unpleasant reality into a world of trifling compensations, or an attempt to avoid the real task in order to hide as much of his personality as possible.

The minute details, *ddd*, are frequently escapes from reality into the realm of fantasy, such as some children love to indulge in.

While the absence of these responses merely denotes a lack of deeper interest in the task and a trend to be readily satisfied with the commonplace and obvious, their excess is clinically more important, and should be interpreted along the lines indicated.

## THE WHITE SPACE RESPONSE, *S*

This also is an unusual response, and as such is grouped with *dd* and *ddd* for purposes of assessing the patient's mental approach to the task.

But it has also a significance of its own. In selecting a white space for interpretation the patient has reversed the task he was set. It may be argued that a very keen or an obsessional personality, aiming at exhausting all the possibilities of the card presented to him, will finally relinquish the blot itself and try responding to the white spaces. This does happen sometimes, but only rarely. In my experience a number of processes can induce the selection of white spaces.

1. Infantile adaptability of vision may produce such reversals more easily than the more rigid adult fixation of attention on the actual blot.

2. A sequence of ideas expressed as mixed responses may gradually lead from the blot to the white. This also is particularly frequent in children. The blot, or part of it, is likened to a map, a seashore or an island, with the addition that 'all that (viz. the white) is sea'. In Card I the central white spaces are often interpreted as lakes on a map. The patient's attention having thus been drawn to the white as part of his picture, he will sometimes follow this up, with a space response proper. 'Houses' with white spaces for 'windows', or 'cliffs' and 'rocks' with caves through which one can see the sea or the sky[1] are also common responses which tend to break down the barrier

[1] See p. 127.

between blot and white space. There is a suggestion of opportunism about such a development of the responses; the patient has let himself be led astray from the task proper by the opportunities offered by the white spaces.

3. The $S$ response may be the expression of stubborn perseverance when blot interpretation has failed to furnish further material.

4. $S$ responses may occur at any time spontaneously out of an unconscious desire to oppose the instructions received. They are the expression of a general opposition trend, a rebellion against the world and its authorities. Rorschach discovered this tendency among many of his patients who furnished this kind of response, and it should be regarded as the most important of the various deductions one can make. An opposition trend is vital for stubborn perseverance 'against all opposition', for opposition stipulates a restraining barrier against which the effort is directed. There is a perseverance which profits by experience and, having failed one way, tries another way to reach the goal. The stubborn individual is one who continues to employ the same method to achieve victory, rather than to adapt new methods to his purpose. There is a double element of self-will expressed in stubbornness, the self-will towards the goal and the self-will in the continued use of the method employed for that purpose.

It has been claimed that $S$ responses indicate opposition tendency in the extratensive personality, and stubbornness in the introverted. (These personality types will be explained in the next chapter). There is reason to believe that opposition may be equally part of the one type of personality as of the other, and that there is very little difference between opposition and stubbornness. The difference arises when the personality has managed to utilize the inherent trend to opposition for a well-directed purpose, like the gradual evolution of perseverance out of stubbornness.

Perhaps one should also take into consideration the nature of the white space to which the response was made, for some, like the central white in Cards II or VII, seem to invite interpretation far more than others.

In practice it is found that many individuals, whom one could only call rebels against society, may never give a single $S$ response in the course of a thirty to forty response record, while others, who appear meek and mild, may give several. A certain trend to opposition is common to all human beings, and becomes pathological only when it ceases to be governed by reason. To make the diagnosis of a definite opposition tendency from the *S* responses, they should be carefully analysed and the various possibilities outlined above considered. For instance, if it is found that an adult has preserved his childhood's adaptability of vision for the reversal of blot and ground, this is undoubtedly clinically significant, while at the age of eight or nine it would be less so. Or, to give another instance, a patient has given no *S* responses to the first three cards, and suddenly does so to Card IV after a failure at a *W* interpretation to this blot: here the patient has suppressed the impression of the threatening male figure, but it has aroused his dormant instinct of rebellion, of opposition, which he then expresses by his choice of white space for interpretation.

# THE PERSONALITY STRUCTURE

Under personality structure we understand the combination of the various responses according to their scores tabulated under this heading. It will be shown in the next chapter how these can be arranged in a graph for the purpose of giving a clear outline of the personality in its essential composition. Here, only the individual response scores will be discussed.

## THE MOVEMENT RESPONSES

Movement responses are the result of a phantasy process. This phantasy may be inadequate or excessive for the purpose of dealing with the problems of reality. Furthermore, this phantasy life may be based on urges and drives from different levels of consciousness.

### 1. *Object Movement, m.*

This is a relatively infrequent response. It is a curious fact that it occurs far more often in connection with an unpleasant than a pleasant feeling tone. Most of these responses are derived from violent colours or from the chiaroscuro, whose significance we shall discuss presently, or else they are directly linked to bizarre thought pictures. The gushing blood or the erupting volcano, the flickering fire, the storm-lashed tree, are familiar responses to coloured blots. The drifting storm-cloud, the whirling waterspout, the rushing torrent, the landscape in an earthquake, all make use of the chiaroscuro, while those bizarre and detached hands that are clawing, isolated fingers that are pointing, or feet that are kicking belong to the realm of mental pathology.

61

In these cases one might speak of *hostile inner forces* prompting the *m* response.

Another series of movements of inanimate objects, however, are of pleasant character: coloured fountains playing merrily, gorgeous fireworks going off, brooks rippling through sunny fields, palm trees swaying in a refreshing breeze, or laughing faces looking out of the blot. Here one would feel inclined to doubt the existence of hostile inner forces if one were not familiar with the outwardly harmless and pleasant pictures of some dreams from which the sleeper may awake in an acute anxiety state with violent palpitations. Undoubtedly these object movement responses can and do occur in normal personalities too, just as dreams are common property, but they should be the least numerous of all the movement responses. We are probably justified in suspecting behind the *m* responses deeply buried unconscious powers which fail to find an outlet or sublimation in that patient. Most of these responses have a dreamlike, symbolic quality which can be analysed and which will reveal hidden sources.

## 2. Animal Movement, FM.

In childhood, the problems of the adult human world are less close to us. Life is a series of instinctive drives, and movement is frequently the expression of joy or an imitation of animals, of an impulse to hop or skip without any other aim than gratification of a desire to move. The pleasure principle dominates the day, and the animal absorbs more of the child's interest than man. Human movement responses are not frequent before the age of eight; animal movements hold the field up to and beyond that age. This is probably less because the child is conscious of a kinship to the animal than because it takes as yet only a superficial or restricted interest in human affairs at large. The animal parallel is an unconscious one.

It is a curious fact that animal responses may amount to half the total responses, yet only a few of them are conceived in motion. Nor is a movement perceived in all those blots which seem most suggestive. Frequently a shape which seems to portray movement is responded to as if stationary while some equivocal part of a blot will produce a distinct impression of movement in the patient's mind. It is as if a pent-up urge of phantasy had to unload itself from time to time irrespective of the suitability of the occasion. This can, of course, be said of all movement responses, but it is particularly striking in the *FM* type.

# The Significance of the Separate Scores

The interpretation given to this response is that it represents *primitive instincts and drives* which predominate in childhood and which persist throughout life, but which gradually become subordinated to the mature drives of conscious adult existence. In childhood they play the predominant role, lying very close to consciousness. Through the years of training and experience they become more and more repressed to a deeper level, while new concepts and urges begin to fill consciousness. The movement responses offer a most interesting insight into the growing child and its personal phantasy life, and to compare the record of a precocious only child of eight years of age, with its mixture of *FM* and *M* responses, with that of an average child of the same age from a large family circle, is very revealing.

Movement responses being the expression of phantasy, one can therefore define the significance of the *FM* response as phantasy which derives its driving power from the primitive instincts of childhood.

## 3. The Human Movement, M

This represents the mature phantasy process of adult life. It appears gradually after the age of eight, when the child has learnt to pay more attention to humanity and has learnt to compare himself with his fellow human beings in many activities. The phantasy life of the adult is full of human movement; the daily press, the books he reads, or the films he sees, are all suggestive of such movement at a conscious, everyday level. If he thinks about human problems at all, he must do so on a phantasy plane which includes movement through space and time. Life is a series of contacts with other human beings, and these contacts stimulate a thought or phantasy process which in turn will become a mental energy which can either consume itself in futile phantasy pictures or lead to creative thought and activity. The young child is essentially an individualist, and the realization that he is only one of a multitude of individuals like himself dawns only slowly on his mind. Maturity means feeling oneself an integral part of humanity as a whole. It is therefore characteristic that so many schizoid personalities and neurotics in whom infantile fixations are strongly preserved, feel themselves to be outside the rest of humanity, isolated and 'different' from other human beings.

We know that no development is sudden, that no change of personality can take place without following the rules of evolution. It would therefore be very surprising if approximately at the age of eight or nine all children suddenly gave *M* responses, of which previously no trace could be discovered. Indeed, it would make one doubt the validity of the test if it suggested so unnatural a development. In actual fact, the gradual awakening of the sense of human kinship and the development of mature phantasy can be clearly traced.

There are two types of early *M* responses which often precede its mature form: one is based on a modification of the movement to little more than an attitude, for instance 'standing', 'lying', 'sitting', 'sleeping', 'kneeling', 'looking', 'talking', 'facing', and similar activities. The other is based on a modification of form perception in order to endow a blot detail of very dubious form with the movement which the patient's phantasy wants to express. The patient—usually a child—chooses for interpretation a minute detail, mostly some tiny spike along an outside edge, whose actual shape is quite insignificant, and endows it with the qualities of a human figure in movement. This movement may in this instance be fully active, for example, 'walking', 'running', 'climbing', 'fighting'. These two preliminary stages of movement perception show that there is an initial difficulty in harmonizing phantasy with reality, and movement perception with form in the ink blot test. The two processes, movement through attitude, expression, or a similar form of restrained action, and movement through selection of minute detail, are not identical. The first is by far the more common, and perseveres into adult life, where these subdued movement responses mingle with the true *M*. It indicates a restrained phantasy life, the tendency to moderate and curtail such mental processes. The second is rarely met with in adults, and shows an excess of phantasy, a trend to confabulation and introversion, in which phantasy can run riot. This process is more closely linked with the fairyland of childhood than with reality. In the first instance, reality in the form of the blot has imposed a restraining hand on phantasy, and the response is cautious. In the second, reality has been forcibly adapted to the phantasy content.

These stages should be of great interest to the psychologist who is dealing with children and young adults.

There is also another *M* response not infrequently given by children: the man riding on a horse or driving a horse and cart. Here animal and human movements are combined into one single picture for which the pictorial basis derived from the blot is frequently very inadequate. Of the human figure only the upper body can be made out, and of horse or cart no more than an upper outline, possibly somewhere a little spike which could resemble the ears of the animal. An occluding hedge or a lane is usually confabulated to this picture to account for the absence of its lower half. This is essentially a confabulatory response, but owing to its co-ordination of small or minute details it seems to point to a somewhat higher level of mental development than the two previously mentioned. It does not seem to have a special significance of its own except in the light of what has been said about development.

The $M$ response proper should express a movement through space. In the last chapter the suggestion will be made that immature $M$ responses should be scored separately and given a lower value in the final assessment.[1] Here, the beginner is advised to score all these responses as $M$ till he is fully familiar with the variations.

The picture of human activity is a reflection of a mature and conscious phantasy process, of the capability to absorb experience and benefit by it or utilize it, to think purposefully about problems, or else to submerge all desire in phantasy pictures. Phantasy in itself may be mature, but it may be misused. The $M$ response reflects the patient's inner life, his mental activities and their level.

## THE CHIAROSCURO RESPONSES
### 1. The K Response

In a person studying the blots for the purpose of finding similarities which could be interpreted as a picture, a peculiar mental attitude must be presupposed in order completely to lose sight of shape and outline and to react only to the shadings and tones of grey at a given point of the proceedings. It is obvious that some inner force is defeating the patient's aims and diverting his attention from those characters of the blot which lead most easily to a response. His eye withdraws from the outline, having failed to fasten on any shape commonly interpreted by other individuals, and ranges over the inner mottling of the blot. Where, in other patients, some line or some blot arouses a memory, that vague, diffuse, grey-in-grey reminds him of a sensation, vague and abstract, which can only be expressed symbolically. Like the $m$ response, the $K$ response has a symbolic significance based on unconscious or semi-conscious

[1] See page 125.

factors of a disturbing or distressing nature. The conflict between two desires, the problem for which no practical solution seems possible, results in a desire to escape from their haunting presence, to forget, to draw a veil over them. The course of time enables the patient to complete such a process, and he can once more give his attention to the immediate problems of existence, while he remains merely dimly conscious of a shrouded mystery, a veiled threat somewhere inside his mind. It is essential for his well-being and peace of mind that this veil be not lifted, that the very shape and outline of the suppressed problem be effaced by a blanket of fog. The result of this process is a vague inner anxiety, a haziness tinged with terror that is no longer attached to any particular problem, but free-floating and elusive. Such a frame of mind could find no more suitable symbolic description than a grey cloud, or dark waters. That inner fog which covers the trouble from which the patient is trying to escape, carries a depressive quality of darkness at times. At others the stress is not laid so much on the inner as on the outer quality, the diffusion and haziness of outline. Dream symbolism finds a close parallel in these responses, and the picture may outwardly be merely shapeless and hazy, yet not particularly unpleasant, and still hide the deepest inner anxiety.

The K response expresses therefore *inner anxiety*, often described as 'free-floating' or 'hazy' to distinguish it from conscious fears and phobias.

The response is not met in personalities of simple structure free from such inner anxiety. It is sometimes found in the more elaborate personalities of the educated or intellectual classes without gross neurotic symptoms. When it is remembered that the more thought is given to the problems of life the more insoluble they frequently appear, it is not strange that some degree of inner anxiety shrouds what has become intolerable to the consciousness of a person of intelligence and the tendency to use it.

As has already been mentioned in the chapter on Scoring and Tabulation, K is frequently combined with m, another response prompted by the 'deep unconscious'. Such combinations merely reinforce their respective significance, the 'hostile inner forces' of m being a common source of the 'inner anxiety' expressed in K.

## 2. The k Response

Human nature rebels against any insoluble personal problem

which is giving rise to anxiety. This anxiety is conscious while the mind is still groping for a solution. It may be found possible to temporize or to find a modification instead of the hoped-for solution. This is an attempt to modify anxiety by a process of reason. The modified anxiety is kept near or at the level of consciousness, and the person tries to deal with it in a reasonable way. *The k response represents inner anxiety in the process of rationalization.*

This does not by any means indicate that this process will be successful. Involutional melancholics, for example, frequently give many *k* responses. And some re-tests show that these *k* responses become partly or totally replaced by *K* responses in cases that show a clinical regression or degeneration.

In the majority of favourable cases *k* follows *K* in the re-test. It is the patient's attempt to deal with his inner anxiety in the light of new experience and knowledge gained through the years. Problems and worries may still remain insoluble and submerged, but the patient has learnt ways and means by which he can bring a modicum of relief to his anxiety.

This reasoning factor which enters into the response is contained in the form element which has been identified in the chiaroscuro. The blot is no longer shapeless and evanescent, but grey-against-grey assumes a stabilizing quality of depth or outline or suggestion of light and shade, in which forms can be identified. Although the general outline of the blot is still either totally ignored or relegated to a secondary position, the 'grey vagueness' has been attacked with the weapon of reason, instead of avoided as in the *K* response.

It is common to find at least two or three main chiaroscuro responses represented in the same record from people of good intelligence. Usually *K* and *k*, or *k* and *FK* occur together, but all three may be represented.

As the *k* response is an intermediary stage between *K* on the one side and *FK* on the other, its prognostic significance can only be assessed with reference to the clinical history. Otherwise it is difficult to tell whether one is dealing with an upward progress from *K* to *k* or with a stage on the descending road to *K*. The possibility of *k* arising independently of *K* as a modified anxiety form of its own must also be considered. For clinical and practical purposes these theoretical questions are not of great importance, however.

These reflections on the nature of the chiaroscuro responses should enable the beginner to distinguish between those selections of inner parts of a blot where light grey and dark grey are clearly separated as areas, as in the 'boot' of Blot IV, or the centre of Card I, and true chiaroscuro, where it is the intermingling of light and dark tones inside an area that stimulates the response. Where these responses make use of such areas on a basis of outline only, they are not chiaroscuro. The latter score should only be used where shades of light and dark inside such an area have been utilized as well, to construct eyes, nose, mouth and modelling of a face for instance.

### 3. The Vista Response, FK

While most responses are based on two-dimensional perception, there are a few which utilize the finer shades of grey to suggest depth to the picture. Such a construction requires a keener eye, a finer observation of reality, and a more accurate reasoning power than the $k$ responses. In the latter the patient makes use of the shading to add detail to his response picture. In some instances he does use them three-dimensionally as in relief maps and the modelling of faces, but here the darker shades merely represent shadows on the surface of one single object, be it a relief map or a face. That shadowy quality is a very characteristic and clinically significant part of $k$, and is quite different from the character of a vista response.

In the $FK$ response the tones are interpreted as spatial depth in the picture, and converging edges of detail are often combined to add to the illusion of, e.g. a view down the length of an avenue of houses or trees. In these responses, form is treated with care and judgment and harmonized with tone.

A person capable of $FK$ responses has not only gained a good insight into himself, but has also learnt to adjust his fears and anxieties to reality and the exigencies of human society. His own troubles have given him an understanding for others similarly troubled. He has overcome or lost the vague inner 'free-floating' anxiety by dealing with it rationally and successfully. Where $FK$ is the only chiaroscuro response, it is probably the last trace of an anxiety period through which the patient has passed at one time of his life.

The $FK$ response is frequently associated with literary gifts or tastes including poetry. It is also commonly given by artists, where the eye for tone is part of the professional equipment, and the response therefore conditioned in a way similar to the medical man's many anatomical responses. But it is far less important to connect any particular response with some special talent, gift, or character trait, than to be able to visualize what kind of process the patient's personality must have undergone in order to be able to produce it. Symbolically speaking, there is also the expression of a longing to look into the future, or of a concern with the future in the vista response. But it is essentially dominated by cool, logical thinking.

*The FK response indicates the finer intellectual faculties and the talent to adapt these to human society.*

## THE FORM RESPONSES, *F*, *F*+, *F*−

The interpretation of the shape of a blot, free from any perception of movement, blind to its colour, and without paying attention to the chiaroscuro, can best be compared with the process of reading. The individual letters do not arouse any emotion nor convey movement, and their tone and colour can be, and is, ignored by the reader. It is a purely intellectual process, in which form-perception and form-interpretation are guided by memory of pictures of similar shapes. It is not the form score *F* which becomes morbid or schizoid, but the content of the response. These two factors must therefore be strictly differentiated. The content of a response may be pathological, yet identified in the ink blot by a mechanical process of reason. For the five-year-old child the task of identifying the letters B, L, O, O, D, will require intelligence and memory alone. Only when he becomes aware of the meaning of those letters may he experience a passing sensation of discomfort. To produce for example, a morbid or a schizoid response content, form perception goes further than it should or is guided by a taste for the macabre or the bizarre. The blot which resembles the rump of an animal is clearly identified, but where another individual would leave it at that, the person with morbid trends will look around for the missing head or a missing leg, and possibly see them in a distant blot and describe the picture now as an animal torn to pieces. Each part, however, was merely identified by its form—(that process of reason alluded to). Or a human figure is spotted, and going out from it, neighbouring parts of the blot identified as wings or further limbs or heads : their identification by their individual forms is a process of intelligence, while their subsequent combination is due to the person's schizoid trends.

The *F* response must therefore not be confounded with the content score or any other character of the same response. *F, Form identification, is a function of intellect or reason.* But this 'reason' has not the significance of 'common sense', or even 'intelligence' in the colloquial sense. In its pure form its quality within the personality is that of a restraining influence on spontaneous mental activities, it is a limiting factor devoid of phantasy or emotion, free from sensual perception or anxiety. This reason is best compared with that 'critical intellect' that enables a child to learn and distinguish his letters. He may learn to form words and read them aloud, but their meaning may pass him by.

This form perception $F$ is an integral part of every personality that is capable of leading an independent existence. It is its framework, stable and solid. If the $F$ response is regarded in this light, not only will the significance of $F+$ and $F-$ as purely intellectual qualifications be readily understood, but also the quantitative factor of having neither too much nor too little of this framework.

'$F$' is called a 'neutral' response, because it lacks that spontaneity which colour or movement perception would lend it. It may occur within a fraction of a second of seeing the blot, and be spontaneous in this sense, but under 'spontaneity' in the Rorschach language, one understands the yielding to an impulse to which sober reason is opposed. Movement perception is such an impulse, while 'sober reason' clearly recognizes that the blot is not moving. The patient's yielding to the appeal of colour is due to a similar impulse when his reason tells him that the shape of the blot is inappropriate to the response he is giving.

In identifying the $F$ response with an intelligent critical faculty one must therefore not see in it an intelligence test factor. It is not possible to use $F$ only by itself for an assessment of the I.Q. These responses form a small part of the personality, and indeed only a part of what other methods are testing as 'intelligence'.

The $F$ response expresses a critical controlling part of the intellect, pure reason which prefers solid facts to flights of fancy or emotional inspirations.

A qualitative distinction is made between form well seen $F+$, and form badly seen $F-$. These qualifications can be directly applied to the significance of the form response: $F+$ suggests good reasoning powers, $F-$ poor ones. $F-$ does *not* mean a low intelligence grade judged by itself. All one can say when meeting $F-$ in a record is that the critical faculties of reason have been impaired or upset by some factor which must be sought by further investigation of the record.

$F+$ is perhaps less labile in its significance: it is always an expression of good reasoning powers and good critical faculties.

## The Significance of the Separate Scores

It has already been mentioned that movement responses, in particular the *M* and *FM* scores, are based on form perception without which only abstract or shadowy movement were possible. It is therefore advisable to take well-seen movement responses into consideration when assessing *F*+ in order to obtain the fullest possible range of the patient's capacity for 'reason'. It is a common experience that phantasy, like emotion, diminishes the critical faculties of reason. The reverse either does not obtain at all or must be very rare. Exceptionally well-seen movement responses have therefore the same value as *F*+, and in the final interpretation may be contrasted with any *F*— that may be found in the record.

### THE SURFACE TEXTURE RESPONSE, *c*

This falls at present into two components, the 'touch-feeling' response, and the 'surface pattern' response. It is as yet uncertain whether these are identical in their significance for the human personality or whether they are distinctive off-shoots from the same root. The character of the blot which has given rise to both types of response is the chiaroscuro, which here does not seem to have any affinity to anxiety.

About the touch-feeling type of *c* response a number of facts have been established and some plausible explanations offered, so that it seems topical to deal with this response first, and as concisely as possible. After that has been done, the problem of the surface-pattern response can be discussed from an established base for comparison.

The touch-feeling response presumes that the mottling of the chiaroscuro arouses in the patient the impression that the blot would not feel like paper, but like some other material, if he should touch it with his fingers.

There is an infantile stage of development when everything must be tested by putting it in the mouth, in order to learn about its qualities or merely in the hope that it may taste good. The oral zone gradually gives way to the digital zone as an authority for investigation, and the child reaches the stage where seeing must be accompanied by touching, that stage, where exasperated parents are wont to say: 'Don't *touch* it—you can *see* it perfectly well.' The development of sensual perception is, of course, greatly fostered by the experience of pleasure derived in this way, and everyone is familiar with those phases of human development where a child can keep himself amused by stroking his skin with a feather or a piece of fur, where he lays his cheek against cool marble, or revels in the sensation of walking barefoot through the grass, and many other experiences through the sense of touch. Education gradually lays a restraining hand on these impulses, and drives these perceptions from the surface into the realm of phantasy, or, in other words, leaves only keen memories of sensual experiences connected with the certain objects.

In the course of development from childhood through puberty and adolescence to maturity, these sensual perceptions can change in several directions. They can degenerate through neglect and so cease to be qualities of importance in that personality. They can become increasingly powerful through many channels of enjoyment being open to them—for instance through food, drink, clothing, games or the finer amenities of existence. They can become repressed after an initial development as a source of pleasure. Or they can be sublimated by that process of maturation of the individual where education offers substitutes for impractical or undesirable outlets.

It is obvious that when those touch-feeling tendencies are still inherent in a personality, they may find expression in one of the responses, and the *c* response offers the best opportunities for this purpose. Its interpretation, as in the case of that of other responses, must fit the actual personality; it is often impossible to decide from the isolated response itself whether it is due to sensuality in the sexual sense or to a sublimation of this instinct in the total personality. One knows the sources from which the response is derived, and one is at liberty to give them their full Freudian significance. But whether these sources are going to develop into an aesthetic quality of tact and an 'awareness' of the presence of other personalities, or whether they will act as the pleasure-seeking impulse of the *bon viveur* or remain on the animalistic level of gross, unbridled sexuality, will depend on the many inner and outer forces which press an individual into a certain mould.

The surface pattern type of *c* response, the 'grained wood' or the 'patterned marble', seem also to be derived from the pleasure principle. But in contrast with the previous type, the sensation here is perceived through the eyes. In its cruder form it expresses the sensuality of the 'voyeur', and in its more refined, the aesthetic or artistic temperament. Patients giving this kind of response have an 'eye for what is pleasing in life'. Occasionally, however, the tone of the response is unpleasant, the impression of the mottling of shades is one of ugliness. One feels inclined to identify such responses with a pessimistic attitude on the part of the patient, as if he had learnt by experience to be on the look-out for nuances in his environment which could threaten his comfort and offend his sensual perceptions. Undoubtedly such reactions are mainly due to repression of the fundamental sources of sensuality, and they are a valuable hint to submerged trouble in the personality of the patient.

It will be seen from these considerations that the interpretation of these *c* responses depends largely upon the skill and experience of the psychologist, and that valuable information can only be gained from them through a careful analysis of all the relevant factors. In distinguishing between *c*, *cF*, and *Fc*, therefore, only an attempt has been made to outline their possible significance.

### The Pure c Response

Here the outer form of the blot has been ignored entirely, and all attention been absorbed by the surface, which may have been responded to as texture or as pattern. In artists or craftsmen the response may be the reflection of professional interest, but in the absence of such a motive one must suspect a form of sensuality that escapes the control of reason and self-criticism.

### The cF and Fc Responses

When 'reason' begins to exert its control over the sensual instinct, consideration of form is added to the response. The transition from the crude *c* to the refined *Fc* is as gradual in the various responses as it is in human nature. But it should not be forgotten that the *F* factor is not merely 'reason' in a qualitative sense implying a superior intelligence, but the force of critical intellect adjusting an instinctive drive to the environment. It deprives the sensual desire of its crudeness, its unheeding animal character. But it does not necessarily change it into an aesthetic feeling. The introduction of the form factor may indicate that the appetite of the senses has become fastidious, or that more elaborate methods have been devised for its satisfaction. Only in the best sense does it signify a sublimation, the replacement of the crude aim by one of high moral value. Quantity as well as quality of the response is of significance here, just as in other response groups—a point which will be discussed in a later chapter.

*Fc* has been defined as 'tact' not in the colloquial sense so much as in the form of an *'awareness of other people'*. I myself have found

73

it very frequently associated with people of outstanding 'tact' and the gift of handling others. I have also found it in cruder personalities in whom tact was difficult to find, but where sensuality in the Freudian meaning was strongly present. And I have met it in the record of people of fastidious tastes who enjoyed the good things of life.

It seems therefore advisable to define all *c* combinations as the reflection of some form of sensuality, and to analyse the particular significance in each individual case from the clinical picture and the total personality which the Rorschach record presents.

## THE PSEUDO COLOUR RESPONSE, *C'*

This response utilizes black, white, and grey in their colour values. Form is usually combined with it, but such answers as 'a patch of snow' for a white space are not uncommon.

When it is remembered that the vast majority of reproductions of drawings and photographs in the daily press, in periodicals and in books, are in monochrome, and that one unhesitatingly identifies the details as representations of variously coloured objects, then it will be realized how strange this response really is. Its appearance means the break with a habit that has been established in school, when black forms on white paper, or white chalk lines on a blackboard were identified with letters and words. The interpretation of a photograph or some monochromatic illustration has become an automatic process, and it is the object represented which suggests its colour, and not the printer's ink or the silver nitrate compound.

In the *C'* responses the patient becomes aware of the colour of the medium which has been used for the monochromatic blots, I, IV, V, VI and VII, and for the Indian ink parts of Blots II and III. The mental process is easily followed where such a response occurs first—and possibly only—to Card II: the introduction of bright red has drawn the patient's attention to the colour factor, and from the idea of 'flames of fire' it is a short step to a 'lump of coal' in a grate. This particular answer is not very rare in connection with Card II. Slightly different is the aspect when the patient does not utilize the red at all, avoids all colour response to that card, and yet reacts to the shades of blackish grey with such a response as 'coal', 'blackened wood', or 'peat'. Here one can follow the trend of repression: the red blots aroused an image of 'fire' in the patient's mind, but this image was at once repressed owing to disagreeable associations, and the attention transferred to the black, resulting in the screen response 'coal' or some such fuel. These kinds of $C'$ responses to Card II are facile and so common that their significance must not be over-rated.

Different is the case where the $C'$ response occurs to Card I or the other monochromes. In this case it is not a second colour which has aroused an emotional response, but the greyish black blot itself or the white ground on which it appears. All colour responses are based on emotion. But black, white, and their intermediate shades are not colour in the proper sense. If the patient responds to them as if they were colour, there must be an equally unusual urge in him which makes him do so. Or else these $C'$ responses represent the overflow, so to speak, of the patient's tendency to respond to colour, and are the intermediary stage between the chiaroscuro responses and those to colour.

There are therefore two types of personalities that give such responses: one whose strong emotional life is not satisfied with the ordinary limits of the range of colours offered for interpretation and is adding black and white to the scale, and the other who fights shy of proper colour, does not respond to it, and treats black and white as substitutes. The former type has an unusually rich and many-sided emotional life, the latter one that is restricted.

The significance which should be attached to $C'$ responses in a record with a good variety of $C$ interpretations ($FC$ and $CF$ in particular) is essentially that of awareness of emotional life. This awareness leads to an enjoyment of sources of emotion in most cases. In contrast to the $c$ responses discussed in the previous paragraph, the pleasure is not sought in sensual but in emotional gratification. This pleasure may be compatible with a healthy attitude to life, an expression of a general 'joie de vivre', or it may be morbid as in sadism and masochism. The instances of such personality pictures are as yet few, and one has to beware of dogmatizing on the interpretation of these responses. For the psychologist it will be sufficient to find here the essential principles with which to work out the solution of each individual problem.

Where the $C'$ responses occur in records devoid of genuine colour responses or with only one or two, leaving the $C'$ responses in an absolute majority, their significance is that of an emotional restriction. The patient feels the common calls of emotion, but is fighting shy of them. He has found his outlet in a guarded reaction to black, to white, or to grey, which do not upset him in the way that colour does. He escapes his emotional responsibilities and problems by repressing them, and creates substitutes on a lower emotional level, a level so low that it is no longer a disturbing influence in him. This type of response is frequently found in persons with an unhappy childhood history, where their affections suffered bitter disappointment. The orphan, the unwanted child, the person disappointed in love early in life, all give this response so often that it has rightly been called 'the burnt child reaction'.

The introduction of the *F* factor into the response modifies it in the same way as in the case of *c* and the case of *C* which will presently be discussed at length. The proportion in which form perception is added to, or dominates, the $C'$ responses indicates the amount of critical thinking, of logical reason, which enters into these 'cautious' unusual forms of emotion.

## THE SIGNIFICANCE OF THE COLOUR RESPONSES, *C*, *CF*, AND *FC*

In contrast to the common interpretation of black on white as a form representing an object either symbolically or pictorially, colour tends to arouse an emotional reaction before an identification with any object is attempted. One is so used to comment on colour as a quality which appeals to the senses or offends them, which is pleasant or unpleasant, that one is apt to forget to what degree colour influences everyday emotional life. Few men are so insensitive to colour that they do not feel a passing pleasure, however slight, in the presence of a colour scheme that they approve. A sunny English garden at its best, the changing reflections of the sky in the sea, or the tints of the glens and lochs of the north, stir emotions in which colour takes a predominant part. It is not logical that a woman should appear more attractive in a frock of one colour than in a similar one of another: it is not a logical, but an emotional reaction. Many people are very sensitive to the colour of the day; they are cheered by a bright sunny sky and mildly depressed by a dull and grey one irrespective of whether they are exposing themselves to the weather or not. Few men are indifferent to the colour of their socks and ties, while women are developing their colour sense to a fine art. The reaction of a bull to red is proverbial, and many children can be rendered irritable by the unsuitable colour of their habitual environment or of their dresses. It is not accidental that red has been chosen to indicate danger. Many emotional reactions to colour may be based on suppressed memories and associations, but some are certainly fundamental, though varying in their significance in the different types of personality. Some people have a liking for soft pastel shades, others for bright colours. Some prefer blues and greens, others reds and yellows. Sometimes a reason for these likes and dislikes can be discovered, more often not. But in all cases the taste is based on an emotional factor.

It follows that a person whose emotions are easily and deeply stirred by colour is to a greater extent at the mercy of his environment than one who is obtuse to it. In the Rorschach test the connection is reversed: a person whose emotional life is not stable will react strongly to the coloured blots.

People who derive emotional stimulation from colour will obviously tend to be in closer touch with outer reality than those to whom the ubiquitous colour means nothing. Contact with reality through the sense of vision stimulates the desire to express, to move about, to act. The *C responses express therefore also a behaviour trend*, which might be called *liveliness of movement or agility*. The influence of control by reason here runs parallel to the interpretation of the response, as emotion. The impetuous, uncontrolled movements of the person giving the pure *C* response, expressing the emotion of the movement, the activities of the emotionally unstable, *CF*, can be logically deducted. While the controlled activities of the *FC* person will be purposeful and utilitarian in character, rather than pure 'joie de vivre'.

## 1. The C Response

To be stirred by the sight of a patch of colour and to respond to it as if it were utterly shapeless, as if colour were its only quality, is an emotional outburst which lacks the critical control of reason. The emotion which has been aroused has led to an association which is spontaneous and unreasoning. It is the equivalent of an automatic action, or of an instinctive drive. Such a process takes place in everyday life when a person 'sees red' and acts upon the promptings of instincts which escape the guidance of reason.

The pure *C* response expresses a *tendency to passion, temper, and uncontrolled emotional outbursts*.

But here again one must beware of attaching the same significance to the response when it is given by artists or other persons whose professional life is spent in handling colours. Such people are undoubtedly more prone to give pure colour responses. Analysis of the personalities concerned shows, however, that it is just among artists that the emotional life is highly developed and very sensitive, so that it is a question whether they respond with *C* because of their vocation, or whether they are artists because their emotion needed an outlet or sublimation.

'Passion' as a motive for the *C* response does not merely refer to violent emotion in the derogatory sense. It frequently means an exceptionally strong love life, which may express itself in singular devotion, loyalty, and self-sacrifice; the power to love and the desire to be loved whole-heartedly. It is important to remember this in the case of children and in child guidance work, lest a child be accused of having a temper, when the *C* response should in fact be interpreted in the more favourable sense.

The apparent duality does not affect the nature of the response. Love and hatred spring from the same source; unbridled hatred or temper is homicidal in tendency, unbridled love suicidal. The response is therefore always an indication of deep and passionate feelings which, when roused, will tend to ignore and escape all logic and reason.

Other types of *C* responses are of less definite significance, and will be mentioned in the last chapter.

## 2. The CF Response

Here the emotional reaction to colour is still so strong that it dominates the response. Colour has aroused associations, usually of a vague, ill-defined object, and the critical faculties have then been called upon to make pictorial adjustment to satisfy form at least to some extent. A blot of green may evoke a memory of leaves, and at second glance its shape has been identified with a tree. An area of pink may suggest flesh, and the form a part of the human body. The colour has determined the nature of the object within wide limits, and form perception narrows these down to a more particular type.

These responses are given by people who follow their emotions more than their reason. They are *emotionally unstable and impulsive*, though not to the degree met with in those giving pure *C* responses. They are inclined to follow their heart rather than their head.

## 3. The FC Response

This response arises out of a primary consideration for the shape of the blot, to which the 'likeness in colour' is added. The head leads and the heart follows. Cool, critical reason has examined the blot and discovered a similarity to some group of objects; the emotional appeal of the colour is then given attention, and that particular object chosen for which the colour is appropriate.

A person proceeding in this way has his emotions admirably under control without being oblivious of their stirrings. In a community of human beings most trouble arises from the uncontrolled emotions of certain individuals. Society demands that emotions be reasonably controlled, and experience teaches the individual the wisdom of obeying the laws of society.

*FC* expresses therefore *essentially social adaptation*. The individual has learnt to fit himself into the group. This is the classical interpretation. But a brief reflection on the nature of the response will show that this is by no means always so. The response expresses control of emotional life by reason. When one is using such terms as 'social adaptation' one is inclined to conjure up the image of a model citizen, who goes out of his way not to offend, who is helpful to others, and an example of virtue and industry. But emotional control in itself does not stipulate any moral quality, though in practice the test result will frequently define the response in that sense. Emotional control is dictated by the reasoning powers present in the individual, and these may be equally as acute in the philanthropist as in the ruthless egotist. The individual may have acquired the necessary control over his emotions for no better purpose than to escape the eye of the law or the censorship of society, and it is not surprising that one finds the response in many youthful delinquents whose pranks have escaped detection for a long time.

The *FC* response has also another significance: it has already been suggested that this group of responses bears a close relationship to behaviour in the sense of physical activity. *FC frequently indicates manual dexterity* or skill in the use of limb and body, such as one would expect to find in the athlete. There is an impulse to physical movement, but this impulse is well directed and controlled by the reasoning faculties and turned to skill. Whether such a person could develop into an artist, a craftsman, or an athlete will, however, depend entirely on whether he has talents or abilities in that direction.

The *FC* response is, generally speaking, one of the most favourable scores of the Personality Structure, and should always be carefully looked for and assessed.

# THE CONTENT

Assessment of the content and its analysis is more properly part of the final interpretation, but there are some types of response to whose content a special significance is attached, and these will be discussed here individually.

## THE ANIMAL RESPONSE

This is the most constantly given response and the one which numerically predominates in most records. This is partly due to the shape of the blots, but if this were the only reason for the response, one would have to assume that, with increased mental perspicacity, a proportionately greater number of animal forms would be distinguished. As, however, the reverse is the case, one must look for another factor.

Animal responses are most numerous in children, in mental defectives, and in neurotics. One feels inclined to see in mental age a common factor for the first two groups. But this could obviously not be extended to the third. The reason lies in the unconscious affinity with the animal, in the inferiority to the average adult population which these individuals instinctively feel, and which leads them to think of themselves as different from humanity. The process is analogous to the one which induces responses of animal movement. It expresses the predominance of animal instincts which have failed to develop to a human level. It is essentially a childhood reaction of mental inadequacy to deal with the problems commonly faced by the adult. In the mental defective this standard is expressed by the term 'Mental Age'. In the neurotic one is dealing with a partial regression to the defenceless attitude of the child, where intelligence fails to deal with the fear-inspiring situation in an adequate manner.

## THE ANATOMY RESPONSE

This type of response *expresses concern with health*. It is natural, and almost inevitable, in the medical and nursing professions, including First Aid personnel. It is frequently found in the records of people who have acquired some degree of anatomical knowledge for their occupation, like the artist and the athlete. It is sometimes produced by events not connected with the patient himself, but which have turned his mind towards the problem of his health, like the death or serious disease of a near relative, or the sight of casualties in battle or from an accident. And it can result from an illness to which the patient has fallen victim and which has left some degree of uneasiness in his mind.

It will be seen from these reflections that the mental precipitants become less and less reasonable the more they are removed from professional interest in ill health. Finally one fails to find any reasonable explanation at all, and the response becomes the expression of *hypochondriasis.* In other words, in some cases the association of ideas can no longer be explained by the conscious content of the mind.

The response must therefore be examined and assessed in relationship to such factors. Their relative number, their special character— e.g. whether scientific or merely morbid—and their relationship to colour will help to decide in each instance whether one is dealing with a justifiable association or with a hypochondriacal trend.

There are many intermediate stages from pride in health to fear of disease, and the clinical picture will range from food fads to neurasthenia and hypochondriacal depression. It is natural that the athlete should take an interest in his health—but so do thousands of other people who do not produce anatomy responses. Nor can it even be said that most athletes respond to the blot in this way. The response occurs when the athlete has become concerned about his health for some reason. It is commonly said of the medical man that the first twinge of pain experienced in his own body makes him at once think of cancer. The doctor deals in illness and disease. The athlete deals in health and fitness. The doctor fears the known, the athlete the unknown. Athletes so responding are usually those who have never previously had a serious illness or even influenza in their lives. They have no experience of the effects that a comparatively harmless complaint like a tonsillitis or an attack of influenza can have on the body. When they recover from such an illness they become aware of an inability to perform feats which formerly were easy for them; if such a man has been out of training for six months or a year he will notice the difference very strikingly, and revert to invalidism because he suspects a hidden illness as the cause of this weakness which to him seems 'unnatural' since his doctor had declared him cured. The psychologist is familiar with the clinical picture of the middle-aged man who was a keen athlete and sportsman in his youth, but has not taken even a reasonable amount of exercise for the last ten

F

or twenty years to keep up a semblance of fitness, and who is now the victim of hypochondriacal phobias.

It seems logical to assume that a certain amount of introspection is necessary before a person will develop an unreasonable concern about his own health. Such a process takes place when that person identifies himself with another person who has suffered illness, accident, or death, and it will be the more effective the stronger the emotional bond is between the two people concerned. On the other hand, there may have been no such mental trauma, and hypochondria arises from a transference of worry about a totally different problem.

The anatomy responses must therefore always be viewed with some suspicion, and only be discarded as 'normal' when their number and quality can be logically accounted for by a 'normal' thought content.

## THE BLOOD RESPONSE

This is a more spontaneous response than the anatomy response, and is frequently associated with acute distress, and based on deep emotional sources. Answers like 'flesh' or 'meat' are its equivalent in a moderated form. The response is more commonly associated with *ideas of violence* in an active or passive concept than with hypochondriasis. It is often given by people who have witnessed gory accidents or been impressed by battle casualties. It points to a process of identification with the victim which has not been abreacted and must be regarded as a neurotic tendency.

## THE RESPONSE OF 'FIRE'

Among the average population before the war this response was uncommon. It increased in winter when the attractions of a cosy fireside naturally stimulated this association, and diminished in summer. Since the war it has become significant through its connection with traumatic experiences involving high explosives and destruction by fire. It indicates a neurotic reaction to these experiences, the presence of an anxiety state on a traumatic basis. Among the children evacuated from heavily blitzed areas it was found in 50–65 per cent during the first few weeks, and then gradually diminished in frequency until it only persisted in those of neurotic predisposition. Its equivalents are erupting volcanoes, gun flashes, explosions of all kinds, and possibly 'fiery sunsets'. Owing to the association of this response with colour its emotional significance is not likely to be overlooked.

# FACTORS RELATING TO QUALITY AND QUANTITY

## THE NUMBER OF RESPONSES AND THE PERCENTAGE OF THE LAST THREE CARDS

The number of responses should be in the neighbourhood of thirty for a satisfactory record; a clinical diagnosis is possible from much fewer than that, but an insight into the total personality is obviously rendered the more difficult the less the material produced for assessment. The distribution of the responses will show whether the patient reacted better to colour or to black and white. It may draw attention to an outstanding 'loading' of a card with responses, or to its exceptionally negligent treatment. A cause for such behaviour should be looked for. It may be due to some rather obvious resemblance in the blot to a sexual symbol to which the patient does not want to respond.

The total responses to the last three cards should amount to 30–40 per cent. Those are the all-colour blots, and the proportion shows whether there is an undue acquiescence to emotional influences or not. Of persons producing 40 or more per cent of their responses to those last three cards it can be said that they are very susceptible to environmental influences, while the reverse applies where the figure is below 30 per cent. Logically, the last three cards should average the same as all the others, and their share be 33 per cent. But Card X has a host of isolated detail which attracts attention, and responses to it are therefore inclined to be more numerous.

## THE SIGNIFICANCE OF THE POPULAR RESPONSE

This indicates a perception of the obvious. The average is 25–30 per cent. Numerical inadequacy suggests that the patient has lost touch with the common aspects and problems of life, either in actual fact or in his mental attitude, that he ignores the commonplace. An excess points to a stereotyped mentality which cannot rise above the commonplace level of thought.

## THE ORIGINAL RESPONSE

This is obviously only given by people who have a store of individual experiences of uncommon character. All people have experiences, but in some these experiences fail to leave any impression.

83

There are the people who travel, yet see nothing worth seeing because they only have an eye for the ordinary, the commonplace, while others can pick out the unusual and store it mentally. A technical response of uncommon character loses a great deal of its originality if it is due to occupational associations of daily routine, while in another person it might be the expression of originality of thought because such associations are lacking.

Originality must be assessed in relationship to the person as well as to the test; nor should the same standards be applied to the labourer as to the explorer or the playwright.

The response shows that a person can think on individual lines, and enjoy some degree of mental independence. *It suggests a power of resistance against what is drab and ordinary in life.*

The 'Original Responses' are most difficult for the beginner to score, as so much depends on the experience gained from a number of records and a clearer conception of the differences involved. Fortunately the response is not so important that any error of judgment is likely to distort the final picture of the personality.

## THE AVERAGE TIME PER RESPONSE

The average time for each response should be approximately one minute. This speed is maintained irrespective of age, but varies according to temperament or clinical picture. If one is taking down a very fast series of responses in long-hand, a good deal of the time taken over a card is due to the writer tending to fall behind in his work. In these records, which are frequently lengthy, few people will be able to write fast enough to adjust their speed to the actual pace at which the responses are given, unless shorthand is used. But as no specific significance is attached to this time factor other than on fairly broad lines, this should not cause undue concern. Many hypomanics and keen normals reduce this time average to half, while it may be doubled in states of depression. By itself it is not a reliable criterion, since mood, attitude towards the test, and other personal factors may influence it. It should be read in conjunction with the rest of the scores and interpreted only with other factors in the whole framework of the personality.

## TIME ELAPSED TILL FIRST RESPONSE GIVEN

Here one is trying to discover whether the coloured cards have produced a time-lag or not. Rorschach believed at first that the neurotic would hesitate longer before responding to the coloured blots than to the monochromes. In actual fact many pronounced neurotics will respond more quickly to the coloured cards than to the others. There are three ways in which the delay in the response time may show: delay at the first introduction to colour in Card II, delay at the sight of the first all-colour card, VIII, and a delay expressed in the sum of the reaction times to the five coloured cards as compared with the sum of that to the monochromes. This delay was called 'colour shock' by Rorschach. It occurs sometimes in one of the above forms and should then be compared with the total picture. This time-delay is used in a formula for colour shock which will be mentioned in the next chapter.

## ADDITIONAL RESPONSES

These have no significance other than that expressed by their scoring, which may show new tendencies or reinforce those already present.

# THE CHARACTER OF RESPONSE

## CONFABULATION

The tendency to weave stories around the main features of a response essentially denotes phantasy and the tendency to revel in it. Such people readily deceive themselves about reality, particularly unpleasant reality. It is more common in childhood, when phantasy is called upon to help bridge the gap that separates it from adult life, than later. It should be regarded as a sign of childhood fixation, unless clinical factors suggest a worse diagnosis.

## THE MORBID RESPONSE

The significance of this type of response lies in its connection with a pessimistic attitude to life or with an acute psychic trauma, mostly of the battle casualty kind. It is closely allied to the Anatomy response in character though it does not seem to express the same degree of hypochondriacal concern with health. It is frequently associated with sadistic or masochistic tendencies. Each case should be assessed individually and the 'morbid turn of mind' interpreted in conjunction with the total clinical picture. Generally speaking the response often expresses sadism in the extratensive type of personality, and in the introvert type a leaning towards masochism. In the form of pessimism it is perhaps more frequent in the introvert personality.

## THE SCHIZOID RESPONSE

While the average person draws on reality for material to associate with the blot, there are a number in whom the picture stimulates more phantastic creations. These are obviously people with a facility for dissociating themselves and their ideas from reality. They can bridge the gulf between fact and fiction without difficulty. Where the average person tends to cut down the area of blot to fit a mnemic association, the other manages to fit an interpretation to any area by drawing on his imagination.

Such a process is natural in artists and writers who would be unproductive if it were lacking. Its significance is therefore closely related to the creative outlet which is available for this phantasy. The main characteristics of the schizophrenic drawing are its lack of reality and the tendency to fill every available space with fanciful designs. In the interpretation of the blot the process is reversed; every part of the blot appears to have some significance, and their border lines are so indistinctly perceived that several parts are harmonized into one single phantastic response. *The Schizoid response expresses a schism in the personality which enables it to live at one and the same time in reality and in fiction.* In a mild form this is no more than an infantile remnant, the gift of wishful thinking common to all children, the talent to shape ideas into clear mental pictures. In a more pronounced form it becomes a projection in consciousness of dreams intricate in their use of the material, dimly symbolic, and vaguely disturbing. Ordinarily the waking mind is incapable of constructing a dream scene of a more complex type than a pure wish fulfilment. But the ink blots can supply the necessary stimulus for processes of symbolism, contraction, and affiliation of details or their imposition on each other. Such a mechanism is found in florid form in many psychotics, particularly the schizophrenics.

The schizoid response varies therefore in quality from a childish play of imagination to the typical schizophrenic product. It varies also in quality from one or two such responses to a considerable percentage. It is perhaps the one response which demands more discrimination than any other, for in a simple, unimaginative personality even a few moderately schizoid answers may point to a latent schizophrenic process, while in a more complex one a good many strongly schizoid characteristics may be compatible with mental health. It should always arouse suspicion, and its significance in each particular case be elucidated by a consideration of the total personality. It is seldom absent from the schizophrenic record.

## REMARKS

These are of significance for assessing the patient's attitude towards the test. They may express pleasure, disgust, interest or a dilatory approach. Their content may be of analytical importance and show secondary associations or repressed memories. They may reveal a particular attitude to colour by commenting on this factor and thus add to our knowledge of the patient's emotional life. They are abundant in the individual who is fonder of hearing his own voice than of applying himself to a task which tends to restrict volubility. They frequently express nervousness and apprehension of the test, or an attempt to hide these feelings. They are usually characteristic of the personality, and worthy of attention.

## EXCLAMATIONS

These are remarks in a more explosive form. They are particularly significant where they occur at the sight of colour owing to the implication of emotional stimulation. Much of what has been said on the subject of 'Remarks' also applies here.

## QUESTION FORM OF RESPONSE

This *denotes an inner uncertainty*, and a dependent nature. The patient is unable to rely on his own judgment, and craves for confirmation and approval of his ideas. He is inclined to lean on others in life, and to be hesitant and irresolute in his behaviour or thinking. Broadly speaking, it expresses irresolute behaviour in the extratensive type of personality, and the equivalent mental quality in the introvert type. It is common in children and shy adolescents, and less often met with in adults. It can be ignored as an isolated instance in a record, but when numerous it must be interpreted as indicated. Such negative answers as e.g. to Card III, lower *D*: 'It isn't a fish, is it?' should also be classified as 'Question' responses.

## SEXUAL CHARACTER OF THE RESPONSE

Sexual responses are usually only given by those who feel no embarrassment in the presence of the person giving the test. They are far more frequently given by men than by women, and by adults than children. They are of small significance in medical personnel, unless excessive in numbers or otherwise outstanding. In the neuroses and the psychoses they occur as part of the mental content, and often point to repressed instincts whose presence the patient may emphatically deny. Their homosexual character may point to auto-erotic trends or homosexual interests, while a few heterosexual responses in individuals feeling at ease during the test and free from repression must be regarded as normal.

There are some cards which stimulate such responses more readily than others. Phallic symbols are most easily recognized in the upper central 'spearhead' of Card II and the elongated upper portion of Card VI. Female sex organs are often identified in the top part of Card IV and the lower central *d* of Card VII. An acquaintance with these details enables one to understand otherwise inexplicably long hesitations on the part of the patient before responding to them. Sexual responses are frequently avoided, but the patient returns repeatedly to these details and produces several indifferent or at best merely symbolical interpretations. He may find his attention attracted by them each time he turns the card, and finally remark on his inability to recognize in it any similarity to an actual object; or he may look upon it for a while in disgust and then reject the card as meaningless. In children and adolescents such behaviour is not rare, and may be the only indication of some sexual conflict, particularly when a heterosexual interest is suggested by the blot. Where sexual responses abound, the content of the patient's thoughts are obvious. But in the young a negative answer is frequently just as revealing as in the case of a boy of eleven who rejected the first three cards with symptoms of great emotional stress, refused to glance at another, and threatened to inform his mother that I was showing him pictures she would not allow him to look at.[1]

## REJECTION

The rejection of any card on the grounds of inability to respond to the blot does not occur in the normally balanced adult. It may be

---

[1] C. J. C. Earl rightly warns against rigidity in the interpretation of disguised sexual content. See his 'Note on the Validity of Certain Rorschach Symbols', *Ror. Res. Exch.*, Vol. V, No. 2. Ap. 41, pp. 51–61, where special reference is made to sexual symbolism in unstable boys of the age of 13–15.

due to a poverty of ideas as in the dullard and the lower grades of mental defect, or to a neurotic reaction, when unpleasant associations are aroused which the patient can only escape by rejecting the whole card. It is often met with in the psychoses, where touch with reality has been lost or the power of concentration impaired, both in the functional and the organic reaction types.

It is rare in healthy children above the age of four and should never be accepted as 'normal' above the age of six.

*A rejection signifies an abnormal mental process*, which will reveal its nature in the analysis of the total record and the clinical picture presented by the patient.

## THE SIGNIFICANCE OF TURNING

The way of handling the card and turning it to inspect various aspects of the blot, is characteristic for each patient. Turning may be completely lacking in mental defectives and depressive psychoses. It is occasionally very restricted in some neuroses.

It may be excessive in fidgety individuals, in many neurotics and 'normals', in hypomanics and other psychotic conditions. It may be due to a spate of associations among which the patient is unable to make his choice and rapidly proceeds to a new position of the blot in the hope of finding a more equivocal picture. Or it may arise from a state of perplexity in which the patient dimly senses associations he is unable to formulate and is trying to escape by turning the blot another way, repeating this process many times.

Turning frequently betrays a trend to opposition when the patient turns the card upside down as soon as it has been handed to him.

The purposeful way in which an intelligent and co-operative person will turn the cards is in obvious contrast to the aimless turning practised by those who are taking no intelligent interest in the proceedings. Malingerers will often turn the blot many times before finally giving a guarded response.

In itself the turning of the blot has no single specific meaning, but in conjunction with the total aspect of the personality it helps to deduct certain qualities. It should also be observed which blots elicit an outstanding amount of turning, or its reduction, as this may help to decide a problematic emotional reaction or some latent sexual drive.

# 5

# THE ASSESSMENT OF THE PERSONALITY

The interpretation of the record consists of a marshalling of all the facts that have presented themselves in the course of the test into a uniform personality image.

It is obvious that a greater insight into a personality is obtained when the record is comprehensive than when only ten–twenty responses have been produced. Co-operation on the part of the patient is important because it encourages spontaneity and fuller description of the responses. A surly patient will often respond with a single word and refrain from mentioning movement or colour even when he has been influenced by them in his choice. It is in cases of this description that a subsequent inquiry with a view to receiving fuller information is most desirable. A record which shows one odd movement response at the one end of the scale and a single colour response at the other does not permit of an assessment of the basic personality or give a reliable picture of the patient's emotional or phantasy life. Such test results leave too much to conjecture and are useless for purposes of character analysis. But they are still of use in connection with any specific clinical picture for diagnostic purposes.

In the assessment one tries to enucleate the basic personality, to discover the traits which have been added to it, and to predict behaviour under given circumstances. Qualities which are rooted deeply, which are fundamental and universal, are claimed as basic. They give rise to certain configurations of the scores which are characteristic for particular age-and-sex groups. The significance of life is that it shapes and develops the personality which should be enriched by every new experience that it brings. Within the limits set by congenital factors the personality can therefore undergo considerable changes in the course of a lifetime, and it is difficult to define any particular aspect of the Rorschach record as basic and unchangeable.

Apart from the gradual evolution of the personality there are also minor changes of a less permanent nature due to temporary disturbances of the mental or emotional balance. But these are seldom sufficiently pronounced to affect the total picture. It must always be remembered that the test is more closely connected with the deeper strata of the personality than with the conscious content, and that such passing disturbances will not often find expression in the record unless unconscious elements are also upset by them.

In view of the great number of factors entering into the assessment it is necessary to follow a definite plan, and to group them under convenient headings. The beginner will find it useful to prepare an assessment table on which the most important relationships between various scores are laid down, where he can survey the essential facts before arranging them into a personality picture. It is also a good practice to test the validity of some of the best-known formulae by completing them in each case irrespective of the clinical picture under consideration. On the tabulation here reproduced the various items are arranged in a way that seems to help the memory rather than the actual interpretation. Figures for 'normal average' have been inserted in brackets to spare the beginner the trouble of having to look them up in a book when his memory fails him. The tabulation is headed by a graph, the 'Personality Structure', in which values corresponding with a theoretical 'norm' have been inserted to illustrate the main points. If ruled foolscap is being used a convenient way is to draw the base line on the eleventh line from the top, and to allocate five scoring units to each space. '*F*' being usually the highest score, this arrangement will allow for fifty *F*'s being built up upon the base line, a number which is commonly not exceeded.

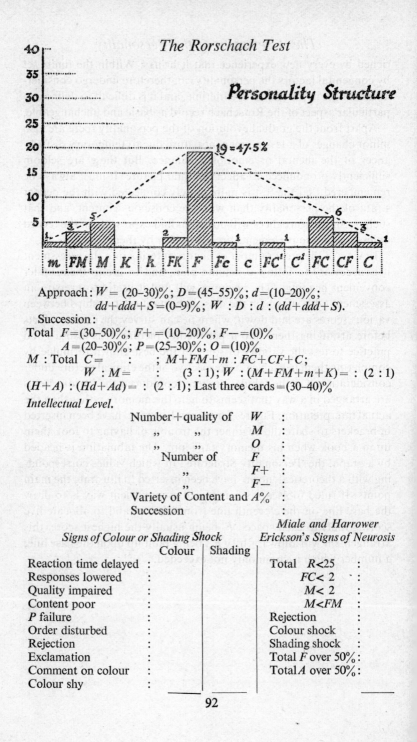

*Personality Structure*

Approach: $W = (20–30)\%$; $D = (45–55)\%$; $d = (10–20)\%$;
$dd + ddd + S = (0–9)\%$; $W : D : d : (dd + ddd + S)$.

Succession:

Total $F = (30–50)\%$; $F+ = (10–20)\%$; $F— = (0)\%$
$A = (20–30)\%$; $P = (25–30)\%$; $O = (10)\%$
$M :$ Total $C =$ : ; $M + FM + m : FC + CF + C$;
$W : M =$ : (3 : 1); $W : (M + FM + m + K) =$ : (2 : 1)
$(H + A) : (Hd + Ad) =$ : (2 : 1); Last three cards $= (30–40)\%$

*Intellectual Level.*

| | | | |
|---|---|---|---|
| Number + quality of | $W$ | : | |
| „ „ | $M$ | : | |
| „ „ | $O$ | : | |
| Number of | $F$ | : | |
| „ | $F+$ | : | |
| „ | $F—$ | : | |
| Variety of Content and $A\%$ | | : | |
| Succession | | : | |

| Signs of Colour or Shading Shock | | | Miale and Harrower Erickson's Signs of Neurosis | |
|---|---|---|---|---|
| | Colour | Shading | | |
| Reaction time delayed | : | | Total $R < 25$ | : |
| Responses lowered | : | | $FC < 2$ | : |
| Quality impaired | : | | $M < 2$ | : |
| Content poor | : | | $M < FM$ | : |
| $P$ failure | : | | Rejection | : |
| Order disturbed | : | | Colour shock | : |
| Rejection | : | | Shading shock | : |
| Exclamation | : | | Total $F$ over $50\%$ | : |
| Comment on colour | : | | Total $A$ over $50\%$ | : |
| Colour shy | : | | | |

| Piotrowski's Signs of Organic Lesion | | Hertz' Signs of Hysteria | |
|---|---|---|---|
| Total $R<11$ | : | $F\%$ low | : |
| Total time increased | : | Dilatation | : |
| Few $P$ | : | At least 1C | : |
| $F$—increased | : | CF>FC | : |
| $M<2$ | : | $\Sigma C>M$ | : |
| Colour naming>1 | : | FM>M | : |
| Perseveration | : | | |
| Impotence | : | | |
| Perplexity | : | | |

# THE BASIC PERSONALITY AND THE GRAPH

This term applies chiefly to the proportion of $M$ responses to colour responses. Rorschach called this the '*Erlebnis Balanz*', the balance of experience. The proportion is established by counting each human movement response, $M$, as 1, and adding up all colour responses by giving them different values: $FC=0.5$, $CF=1$, $C=1.5$. Persons in whom $M$ predominates—that is mental activity and phantasy life—belong to the *introvert type*, while those with more colour than movement responses are *extratensive*. The latter term was created to avoid confusion with Jung's 'extravert' type of personality.

The graph enlarges this primary picture and allows of a rapid survey of the personality structure. The actual proportions of the spontaneous responses—movement, shading, and colour—to the centre column of pure reasoning expressed as form reveal at a glance the general attitude to life. Where $F$ is below 50 per cent there is a good measure of spontaneity, the person allows life to enter into intimate contact with him and in turn reaches out for experience, emotionally or mentally. But where life instils fear into the deeper layers of the personality there is a reduction of spontaneous responses, for phantasy or emotion or both fill the person with apprehension and distrust, the $F$ per cent rises above the fifty mark and can reach the 100 per cent. This diminution of spontaneity is referred to as a 'constriction' or 'co-arctation' of the personality. Instead of utilizing all the means of contact with life that nature has provided, only 'cold reason' or intellect is made use of. This means a repression of some natural faculties and an excessive strain on others. It is therefore not surprising to find $F$ per cent between 50 and 100 commonly associated with neuroses and depressive states, in both of which conditions the normal and natural contact with life has been impaired. This withdrawal into a mechanically intellectual approach to life aims at avoiding upsetting emotions and unpleasant phantasies, but can only be successful up to a certain point. There arise situations in life where this protective barrier is broken down and the pent-up spontaneity bursts forth without control, as occurs in hysterical rage or self-centred depression.

In the graph all the important irregularities of the personality structure attract attention. In the diagram a tentative attempt has been made to construct an 'ideal' graph of 'normal' proportions. Its purpose is to show how the values rise from the two ends towards the reasoning centre, that central control which should exercise its authority over phantasy and over emotion, yet leave them enough freedom to develop for the purpose of enriching the personality. It will be seen that the least controlled responses of phantasy and emotion are at the ends, but there are gaps on either side between $M$ and $F$ and between $F$ and $FC$, which have to accommodate the shading responses. The graph has therefore seldom the shape of a simple curve rising to a peak in $F$ and falling again. Only the end sections, $m-M$, and $C-FC$, behave in this orderly fashion, while the values for $K, k$, and $FK$, and for $C', FC', c$, and $Fc$, should always remain at a lower level than $M$ and than $FC$ or be altogether absent. The best method is to examine the graph first for the relative size of the $F$ column and then for the rise towards it in the movement and colour columns. Then the shading columns are scrutinized on both sides of $F$, and the significance of the less usual responses assessed.

# THE MENTAL ACTIVITY

## THE MENTAL APPROACH

The mental approach is expressed in the proportion in which whole-blot responses appear in relation to major and minor detail ones. A person is most favourably equipped for life if he has a keen eye for a problem as a whole, and enough common sense to recognize in it its main component factors. In addition to this, he should be sufficiently observant to take in outstanding smaller details and to pick out a few unusual aspects as well. Expressed in single figures this proportion should be in the neighbourhood of 3 : 6 : 2, the last figure comprising all $d, dd, ddd$, and $S$ responses. (The tabulation shows the wider range of proportions.) This normal average relationship is represented by the formula

$$W-D-d-(dd+S).$$

Where any of the components exceed the average or fall short of it, the letter is either underlined or put in brackets in the following way according to the amount by which the figures deviate from the average:

| $W$: | | $D$: | | $d$: | |
|---|---|---|---|---|---|
| Less than 10% | $= ((W))$ | Less than 30% | $=((D))$ | Less than 10% | $=(d)$ |
| 10–20% | $= (W)$ | 30–45% | $= (D)$ | 10–20% | $= d$ |
| 20–30% | $= W$ | 45–55% | $= D$ | 20–30% | $= \underline{d}$ |
| 30–45% | $= \underline{W}$ | 55–65% | $= \underline{D}$ | 30–40% | $= \underline{\underline{d}}$ |
| 45–60% | $= \underline{\underline{W}}$ | 65–80% | $= \underline{\underline{D}}$ | 40–50% | $= \underline{\underline{\underline{d}}}$ |
| Over 60% | $= \underline{\underline{\underline{W}}}$ | Over 80% | $= \underline{\underline{\underline{D}}}$ | Over 50% | $= \underline{\underline{\underline{\underline{d}}}}$ |

| $dd+S$: | |
|---|---|
| Less than 10% | $= dd+S$ |
| 10–15% | $= \underline{dd+S}$ |
| 15–20% | $= \underline{\underline{dd+S}}$ |
| 20–25% | $= \underline{\underline{\underline{dd+S}}}$ |
| Over 25% | $= \underline{\underline{\underline{\underline{dd+S}}}}$ |

Rorschach assumed that $W$ responses pointed to a tendency to interest in the abstract. This interpretation is essentially accurate, as long as the clinical picture of the case and the total relationships of the approach are taken into consideration. 'The abstract' refers not only to philosophical speculation but it also includes all the primitive conceptions and simple commonplaces of existence. The significance of the $W$ responses is therefore ambivalent, and may equally well coincide with high as with low intelligence.

In an adult, the person absorbed in abstract problems is commonly suspected of being impractical. The balance of the average approach shows that any significant increase in the $W$ percentage must diminish the $D$ output. Very occasionally one finds a total absence of all small and unusual detail responses, and the $W$ score has grown to 45 per cent while $D$ is still within average limits at 55 per cent. But this 'normal' value for $D$ is fallacious. It is not the absolute figure that matters, but the proportion between the scores. If the $W$ percentage has reached 45 it is in excess of the $D$ score even if the latter is still 55 per cent. That suggests that any excessive pre-occupation with the abstract problems of life must diminish the tendency to use practical common sense. Empirically this seems to be the case. Personalities whose existence is guided by abstract ideas which are not founded on personal experience but which were mechanically adopted in childhood and unquestioningly preserved, show an increase of $W$ at the cost of $D$. Many of these people get into difficulties when life puts before them the alternative of using their common sense or following absurd precepts which have become a habit.

That mental defectives are prone to produce many $W$ responses is not due so much to their leaning toward the abstract as to simplicity of thought as in the case of the young child.

Neurotics as well as psychotics frequently show an Approach picture characteristic of a certain phase of childhood and in those cases it is seldom difficult to find the childish outlook on life expressed in behaviour and mentality. In particular does this apply to the so-called 'fixations' at some stage of childhood development.

It is a good practice to examine the $W-D$ proportion first and to draw a conclusion with regard to the quality and quantity of abstract thinking and to common sense, and then to view these in relationship to the rest of the approach figures.

The presence of many $dd$ and $ddd$ responses arouses the suspicion that the person is trying to find an escape from the real problems of life by courting petty interests. In 'petty' moralists, this picture is often associated with an increase of $W$ at the cost of $D$, while in the 'petty' delinquents the $W$'s are diminished while $D$ remains about average. These examples are merely illustrations of possible interpretations, and do not imply that a diagnosis of delinquency or a trend to moralize should be deduced from the Approach combinations.

The Approach represents a mental attitude and should be treated as such on broad lines until the rest of the personality has been unravelled. Once that has been achieved it should be reconsidered in the new light shed on the personality and utilized to complete the picture.

# The Assessment of the Personality

## THE PROPORTION $W : M$ AND $W : (M+FM+m+K)$

Normally the proportion of $W : M$ should be 3 : 1 in absolute figures, not per cent. $M$ represents a mental activity, a phantasy process by which experiences are linked together, irrespective of whether these have been personal experiences or obtained by proxy through information. In its simplest form, phantasy is a day-dream. But there are inner and outer driving powers which enter into this phantasy life and give it a purpose. Instead of the day-dream appears constructive thinking, and the pictures supplied by phantasy are arranged in such a pattern that their final result produces the solution of a problem. Facts are marshalled and conclusions drawn which serve to enrich the personality and increase the capacity for abstract thought. Personal experience without that process of phantasy which seeks an explanation for the events would lead to a conditioned reflex. Mental activity of a higher order is required to convert experience into an abstract concept, the discovery of the law of cause and effect.

It has been found that the proportion of 3 : 1 for $W : M$ represents the most favourable relationship between capacity for abstract thought and phantasy life. $W$ responses are at least three times as easy to produce from the blots as human movement responses. An intelligent person will tend to select among the possibilities and only be satisfied with good quality $W$'s, thus reducing their relative number, while the mature phantasy will produce 3–4 good $M$ responses. When it is remembered that the last three cards and in particular Card X, do not encourage whole blot responses, the proportion of 9 $W$'s to 3 $M$'s will appear quite logical. These relationships are strictly bound to the ink blots used, and are empirically arrived at; apart from the test the figures would be meaningless.

An excess of $W$ suggests a rather shallow, superficial creation of ideas, while a diminution points to an insufficiency of creative thought in comparison with the phantasy life present. If there is a normally developed phantasy life—expressed in the number of $M$ responses—then it must lead to creative thought and be absorbed by the tasks set by human existence, otherwise there is redundant phantasy and the tendency to day-dream. On the other hand, abstract ideas may have been derived from the outer world without any basis on a personal thought process, they have been accepted but not rationalized. This type of mentality is expressed in the $W$ excess, and the proportion between $W$ and $M$ suggests how far individual thought enters into it. The $W$ responses within normal limits, but the $M$'s reduced indicates poverty of phantasy life, possibly due to an extratensive disposition. This type of person will not be capable of original mental creation of the kind required for instance for a career as an author.

The proportion $W : (M+FM+m+K)$ compares the total mental output with the total products of non-emotional spontaneity. It should not exceed 2 : 1, but may be somewhat less. $M$ should be about double the number of $FM$, while $m$ and $K$ are commonly absent in the average normal individual who does not lay claim to being 'highly strung' in some respects. Where the proportion rises to 1 : 1, there is either an unbalance of $W : M$ or the immature forms of movement and the inner anxiety response $K$ are in excess of the normal adult record. It has been pointed out already that in children the $FM$'s are usually more numerous, so that a 1 : 1 balance is not uncommon.

$M$ should at least equal $FM+m$; if this is not the case, then one must draw the conclusion that phantasy life has not altogether matured, and that primitive instincts and hostile inner forces have remained hidden from consciousness. Primitive instincts are always present but they should only find an outlet through conscious utilization, that is, they should be directed by deliberate thought. Where the phantasy life is inadequate to deal with them, either because it is too restricted or because those instincts are excessive, valuable sources of energy are allowed to run wild. The aim of human evolution, conscious sublimation and conscious utilization of instincts, has not been reached.

# THE INTELLECTUAL LEVEL

The Rorschach Method is primarily a qualitative instrument and therefore not readily adaptable for quantitative assays. But it would be disappointing if one were not able to arrive at a reasonably accurate assessment of the intelligence level in the course of the analysis of the record. There are a number of adjustments to be made for exceptional cases, and the formula in the tabulation of Relationships cannot be handled as a rigidly standardized scheme. Nevertheless, the I.Q. in records without gross abnormality can be worked out to within $\pm$ 5 per cent of the Stanford-Binet Test as applied by Terman and Merrill.[1]

## NUMBER AND QUALITY OF *W*

The number is found by giving the ⅋ a half-value in the sum-total. It should be within the proportions laid down for the approach. The quality of the *W* responses is then examined: how many are poor—(rocks, trees, seaweed, clouds, squashed beetles, etc.) how many are popular (*P*), how many just average—bats, butterflies, skins, and the host of commonly encountered responses, and how many are 'superior' in quality of content and form. It is an analysis which requires a good deal of consideration, and the beginner will often feel at a loss what marks to give. It is a good plan to consider every *W* as average which is not 'very good' or 'very poor'. The more specific the object identified and the closer its resemblance to the blot, the nearer one finds oneself to the 'very good' mark. Objects without definite shape or with many possible shapes point towards the 'poor' mark. The *W*'s are thus sorted into three groups, $W-$, *W*, and $W+$, and the balance drawn. A number can be given to the result, or merely the proportion recorded for the final summing up of the intelligence level.

## NUMBER AND QUALITY OF *M*

*M*, representing capacity for normal motive phantasy, is an important factor in the general intelligence. The average number of *M* responses given by normal adults is 3–4. Before the age of eight, *M* is rare, and from that age on it makes a gradual appearance, being at first represented by expressive poses or linked with minute details of the blot. Such forms of *M* can be used as an index of the mental age, provided this fits the total picture of the personality, and in particular the total aspect of the intellectual level. It must be remembered that these immature *M* responses are the transitional stage from *FM* to *M*, and that a person driven by primitive instincts will show a preponderance of *FM* responses. The immature *M* forms are therefore merely an indication of immaturity or regression of phantasy life, and not a purely intellectual factor. If all other factors point to a good intelligence, such *M* forms point to immature inner

[1] Terman, L. M. and Merrill, M. A.: *Measuring Intelligence: A Guide to the administration of the new revised Stanford-Binet Tests of Intelligence.* London, 1937.

driving powers, without materially prejudicing intellectual capacities of the kind assessed as I.Q. by the usual methods.

Immature $M$ responses should be rated with half $M$ value. Such are those linked with minute detail, where the patient fails to discern movement in those major parts of the blot whose shape can be reasonably identified with a moving body, and merely projects his phantasy, without any effort of reason or discernment, into ambiguous little knobs and spikes; immature $M$ responses are also those expressing merely a pose, because phantasy is inadequate though discernment of form is satisfactory.

A human movement response should be vigorous or represent at least a normal action. It should furthermore be reasonably appropriate for the part of the blot selected by the patient, in other words, the form perception underlying it should be good as well. If those two points have been satisfied, the $M$ response is 'good'. Occasionally one finds an outstandingly good $M$, expressing originality, delicacy of perception and conception, and vigour. Such a response can be given an additional half-value.

It is very difficult to assess the form value of an $M$ response, because the suggestion of movement allows for a greater freedom of shape. It is therefore useful to ask oneself in a doubtful case whether the $M$ was inspired by the blot or merely projected into it by a redundant phantasy. One should hesitate to arrive at the latter conclusion when the record shows no minute detail $M$'s and no $F-$ responses, for it requires considerable practice to see the blot through the eyes of the patient, and he should be given the benefit of the doubt in such cases.

It is a curious fact that many patients will give a vigorous $M$ response to either Card II or to Card III, but not to both. This is particularly surprising when Card II elicited a fairly quick and spontaneous $WM$, and the more suggestive Blot III subsequently fails to do so. It seems to suggest a temporary exhaustion of phantasy after the first outburst, but so far no special clinical significance is attached to this phenomenon.

A good intelligence in a healthy person should produce three good $M$ responses. Assuming the average number of responses for such a personality to be in the neighbourhood of fifty, these $M$'s should amount to 6 per cent.

## THE NUMBER OF *F* RESPONSES, *F*+ AND F −

The quality of these responses being expressed in the symbols, need therefore not be further examined. What is significant is the total of *F* per cent and the relative proportions of average *F*, *F*+ and *F* −. An excess of form responses, viz. their total exceeding 50 per cent of all responses, points to a constriction. Such a reduction of spontaneity may affect the *M* output as well as other responses which do not enter into the intellectual assessment. It is a warning sign that the poor score under the heading of *M* is due to an abnormal mental process, most commonly a neurotic constriction, and therefore not due to a congenitally low intelligence. It points to a process which does not allow the inherent intelligence to be utilized fully.

A richly developed, many-sided personality, should produce a good variety of spontaneous responses at the cost of pure form interpretations. The optimum for *F* lies in the neighbourhood of 40 per cent. Of these an adequate proportion should be *F*+ or outstandingly good form, and none *F* −. As has already been pointed out, the standard for *F*+ assessment varies among the individual Rorschach workers, but as long as this individual standard is adhered to, the final result will be the same, since the whole intelligence estimate is arbitrary and relative. If one observer rates the qualifications for *F*+ so high that the person of average intelligence does not score more than 5 per cent and a university graduate perhaps 15–20 per cent, his estimate of the I.Q. will be as accurate as that of another observer who finds 10–15 per cent *F*+ in the average and 40–50 per cent in the high intelligence groups.

Where *F* − appear at all, they should be more than off-set by the number of *F*+. But here it is important to examine the content of the *F* − responses, for certain abnormal tendencies like the hypochondriacal trend to give anatomy responses, may swell the number of *F* − out of all proportion to the real intelligence level.

If a wide scope is given to the mediocre *F* there will be few *F*+, but even fewer *F* − in the record of a person of average normal intelligence.

## NUMBER AND QUALITY OF 'ORIGINAL' RESPONSES

As in the case of *F*+ and *F* −, the estimate of what constitutes an original response remains largely arbitrary. The figures usually given are 5–10 per cent of the total responses for a good average intelligence. The quality of the response takes into consideration its form—colour—or shading adequacies, or its combination with movement. A good original response should at the same time score $F+$ or its equivalent. The content should be sensible, not merely bizarre. After paying attention to these points it is not difficult to divide the $O$ responses into $+$ and $-$. The latter should not appear in the normal average intelligence group.

The number of satisfactory $O$'s should off-set the number of 'popular' responses. The latter would point to a stereotyped trend of mental life if the person could not rise equally well above the obvious and produce the uncommon. In an intelligent person the Originals should at least equal the Populars.

## THE VARIETY OF THE CONTENT

Theoretically there is no limit to the variety of responses to which the blots can give rise. It is equally obvious that the variety will be the greater the richer the store of the memorial pictures in the patient's mind, and that these riches express an intelligence factor. The simple personality of lower average intelligence is only able to draw from a very limited store of inner experience and will tend to stay in the mental groove into which the first association to the ink blot has led him. Adaptability is a highly significant part of intelligence and the blots offer the widest scope for this quality. For this reason the person of higher education will show a vast diversity of subjects from widely scattered realms of knowledge, while the labourer's scope is soon exhausted. Most important of the content group are the Animal responses, the easiest and therefore the one type of interpretation to which the simple mind will constantly return for inspiration. Once launched on that track that kind of mentality tends to stay on the same course, and the Animal response will rise to 50 per cent and more. This percentage is calculated from the sum total of $A$'s and $Ad$'s. An intelligent person may show about 20–25 per cent. A figure above 50 per cent points to mental defect or an inability to make full use of the inherent intelligence, as in the case of some neurotics who have lost part of their mental adaptability and power of concentration and are therefore forced to take the line of least resistance.

The lower normal intelligence levels produce mostly responses in the Animal, Human, and Object group, with a likely excursion into the realm of geography ('it's like a map'). A highly developed intelligence will tend to cover nearly every realm of interest.

A qualitative factor does not enter into this part of the estimate. It is the variety which matters here, not the abnormality or otherwise of certain responses.

## THE SUCCESSION

The order of succession in which whole blot responses, major detail and minor detail ones follow each other reveals the method and orderliness with which the mind sets to work on a task. It is clear that one cannot and must not expect a rigid scheme which does not allow for exceptions. But there should be a predominant scheme by which the patient proceeds to interpret each blot. Normally one could assume the tendency to look at the blot as a whole first, and then to examine its major and finally minor components. But it must be remembered that the rôle of the blot is not entirely passive. It may upset a preconceived scheme of selection at any moment by giving a powerful stimulation to a process of associations and obtruding upon the consciousness of the beholder a pattern which was not deliberately looked for. Thus after some *W* responses followed by *D*'s and *d*'s a spontaneous response may be given once more to the whole, and, next to a minor detail, or a new aspect of a major one, may suddenly catch the eye. These are spontaneous irregularities normally imposed even on the most methodical succession. The succession is recognized by its predominant trend, which should clearly stand forth among the order of responses to each blot. Most regular should be the initial *W* response. But occasionally a reversal of the process is met with and the *W* responses found at the end of each response series as the expression of final synthesis of integral parts scrutinized first as building blocks which are then assembled to a whole. Such a procedure is not uncommonly adopted by children of four–six years of age, who will call one part of the blot 'a hand', another part 'a foot', then discover 'a head' and then 'a body', and finally call the sum of these pieces 'a man' or 'a woman'. Occasionally there is so much surprise or excitement expressed with that final statement that one cannot doubt the process of synthesis that has been at work. It is, however, obvious that the child has made an unconscious identification from the start, and that the various pieces are instinctively looked for till the suppressed idea can be released.

If the total figure accounts for all or the best part of the blot, one should score only the final *W*.

If a definite method can be identified in the succession of responses to 3–4 cards only, it is called 'loose'; if it is found in 5–7 cards it is 'orderly'; if in 8–9 cards, 'methodical'. Adherence to a *W —D —d —dd* scheme for all ten cards borders upon the obsessional and is called 'rigid'. Where a scheme can no longer be identified the succession is called 'confused'.

An orderly succession is the most common, and agrees with an orderly marshalling of mental faculties. A methodical succession is of a higher order, while a loose one suggests an inadequate control over the mental powers.

It is possible to work out a scheme in which these various intelligence factors are represented as numerical values for an estimate of the I.Q. But this tends to give the assessment a rigid character which it neither deserves nor needs. To sum up the individual results in the form of a 'school report' is quite satisfactory and the margin of error no greater. A simple method consists of giving each factor one of three marks, 'poor', 'fair', or 'good', and to weigh their sum up at the end. Outstanding scores can be given additional value by some qualification like 'excellent'. It is surprising how accurately one is able to predict the results of a subsequent Terman-Merrill after a little practice.

The assessment is inclined to fail when the record shows such abnormalities as are frequently associated with some neuroses. Here one may find a high *F* and *A* percentage with a total lack of *M* responses, and a number of *F* —, so that the picture resembles that of the mental defective or the young child. In these cases the abnormalities justify a different basis for the estimate, and the correct impression of the intellectual level is gained by accepting the most favourable feature of the intelligence tabulation as an index of its level.

For instance, assuming that the quality of the *W* responses totals a 'poor': if it is found that this is due to *K* responses or crude *C*, or to a pathological content like anatomical descriptions based on obsessional concern with the subject rather than on the form of the blot, it is clear that the clinical picture is responsible for the failure, and not a congenital lack of intelligence. The neurotic constriction which leads so often to *M* failure will in most records of average size leave its marks in several places—chiaroscuro responses, *m*, *C*, rejection, colour shock—and thus put the observer on his guard.

For the record of mental defectives such 'excuses' are rare and do not tend to improve the total impression.

It need hardly be mentioned that a ten-response record does not lend itself to an accurate estimate of the intelligence, nor one where most of the items required for that estimation are missing or useless owing to their pathological character. The estimate 'by the most favourable feature' on the list has only very approximate value, and usually falls short of its mark rather than giving an I.Q. which is too high. Estimation of the intellectual level is, however, a practice that should never be omitted in the interpretation of the record. Where it fails owing to abnormalities in the responses or their absence this failure must be harmonized with the total personality. The aim of the test is insight into the personality, and this purpose is furthered by this analysis even if it does not allow of an estimate of the I.Q.

# THE EMOTIONAL LIFE

The emotional life is expressed by the colour responses, and the aim of this part of the investigation is to discover how the outer world affects the patient's emotions, and, secondly, how he deals with the emotions inside himself.

## TIES WITH THE OUTER REALITY

### Colour Affinity

Many people express preference for certain tones of colour. The emotional restraint of blues and greens appeals to some, while vigorous yellows and reds are preferred by others, and responses to favourite colours will predominate over those that evoke a mild distaste. Card VIII is often praised for its 'pastel shades', while another type of personality admires the vitality of the colour scheme in Card X. A deliberately expressed opinion, whether spontaneous or on inquiry, is very often contradicted by the responses given, and reveals conflict between the emotional aim of the personality and the real emotional predisposition. Thus it may happen that someone who has chosen predominantly blues and greens for his responses will afterwards loudly extol the beauty of the reds and yellows indicating a person who is trying to overcome a native shyness and reticence by a bold show of gaiety and false exuberance.

This colour affinity is only of significance when it is unequivocally given expression in the response series. It does not matter whether the response has been made to the form or the colour of the blot, but there must be a clear preponderance of one colour scheme over the other in a ratio of at least 2 : 1, and the responses to the last three cards should not be less than twelve. Where these conditions have been satisfied, the expression of affinity deserves notice, and this is all the more useful if the last three cards have totalled 40 per cent or more of the responses. For if one is dealing with a personality susceptible to environmental influences every additional piece of information in this connection is welcome. Less easy is it to decide whether a predominance of responses to one colour is due to an affinity to it or to a dislike for its contrast colour. The decision may be further complicated by a contradictory 'conscious' preference for colour. It is therefore best to make a note of these points and to wait with their interpretation till the remainder of the emotional life has been analysed, when their true significance should become plain. Speculations about emotional affinity or aversion to certain colours are still rather vague and must therefore be subordinated to the interpretation of the specific colour responses.

## The Proportion of FC : CF : C

The significance of these separate factors has been explained, and it is therefore not difficult to replace the symbols by their actual values and to draw the logical conclusion.

FC is a most desirable quality to possess. It is the perfectly controlled emotional link with outer reality, and reflects not only on the mental outlook but also on behaviour. There should be 3–4 FC responses, or about 10 per cent. They should always be more numerous than the sum of CF+C, and the aspect is the more favourable the greater the difference in the proportion.

The presence of colour responses suggests physical rather than mental activity, and ranges from simple manual dexterity to hysterical outbursts and maniacal hyperactivity. These tendencies are reflected in the proportion of FC : CF : C, for it is obvious that a personality in whom crude, uncontrolled emotional responses to outer reality predominate will be more active than useful. The FC person, on the other hand, feels emotionally stimulated to activity but co-ordinates this impulse through the control of reason and directs it into suitable and profitable channels. The result is social adaptation, the desire to fit into human society as a useful member and to share in its activities, burdens and pleasures. Fondness of sports, frequently expressed in team-work, and skilful use of the limbs commonly go with this type of personality.

How far this aim will be attainable depends on the other qualities of the character, on intelligence, instincts, and maturity. On its own, *FC* represents no more than a tendency, a part of the integral whole, and therefore dependent on the other factors.

Where the number of *FC* is equalled by the number of *CF+C* the person is making a valiant attempt at adaptation, but is liable to be thrown out of balance or diverted from the aim set by events which arouse emotional reactions. Thus this picture may very well apply, e.g. to the golfer who is put off his stroke by an irritating remark or an awkward lie.

### *The Last Three Cards Per Cent*

The significance of this factor has been explained, and it remains only to fit it into the personality picture at this stage. (See p. 83).

## TIES WITH THE INNER LIFE

It has been said above that the most favourable *FC* : *CF* : *C* proportion is still no more than a tendency unless there is a well-organized mental capacity to respond to it. Emotional impulses must result in a phantasy process by which their nature and significance becomes conscious in order to allow reason to take control. The emotional life will become a mere outer reaction if either the capacity for phantasy or reason is defective. Just as the inner instinctive drives must mature through conscious phantasy, so must the emotional urges aroused by the outer world be matured by the same process.

For this purpose the proportion $M : \Sigma C$ is examined. Theoretically it would appear most desirable to find an even balance. In practical life the optimum lies with a slight unbalance either towards the introvert or the extratensive side. Few people are in the fortunate position of leading a life in which their mental powers are exactly as much in demand as their physical activities. The person evenly balanced in introversive and extratensive tendencies does not therefore fit too well into modern life. It is easier to follow a predominant inclination and enjoy the lesser one as a sideline or hobby.

Emotional reactions to outer reality may fail to be absorbed by phantasy or to give rise to mental activity of a mature kind, because that person has not learnt to think for himself. In other words, the *M* responses are totally inadequate for the task of dealing with the emotional impulses expressed by the colour responses. It must be borne in mind that 1 *M* response equals 2 *FC* or 1 *CF*, and that the *FC* response is in itself already under control and for this reason less of a potential danger to the person than the *CF* and *C* scores. An excess of *FC* over *M* need therefore not give rise to alarm, other factors being equal. But where *CF*, and possibly *C* as well, are present, it is important to find a mature phantasy life capable of dealing with these emotional impulses before they lead to impulsive action.

Frequently the *M* responses in patients are abnormally low, while some *FM* are present, possibly in greater numbers than the *M*'s. In such cases it is clear that strong emotional reactions will not be absorbed by the *M* factor, but will stir up the *FM* impulses, of which it has been said that they are primitive and infantile. The conclusion to be drawn is that such a person will behave irrationally and in an immature way when excited or otherwise emotionally stirred. The aspect is worse still if there is an inadequacy of *M* in the presence of *m* responses on one side and considerable pure *C* on the other. In this case the crude emotional reaction is activating the cruder primary instincts, and the behaviour to be expected under emotional stress must be in the nature of the uncontrolled passion devoid of mental guidance, as one finds when a patient is 'behaving like a wild animal'.

It is very instructive to compare the relative value and significance of the components of the introversive with those of the extratensive side:

$$M + FM + m : FC + CF + C$$

The mental reactions to the various emotional possibilities can be readily visualized. Furthermore, the position of *M* in relation to *W* and the intellectual level now links the emotional side with the rest of the personality, and it becomes an integral whole in which the main factors have known values.

## VOCATIONAL ADVICE

These relationships are of particular value when it is intended to give advice on education and the choice of work for which the patient is best suited. The main decisions that have to be made concern the problems of whether he is better fitted for brainwork or for manual occupation, and whether on the creative or the imitative side in either of these. Having assessed the I.Q. and the educational level, the proportion, quality, and character of the *M* responses in relation to the *W* score will allow a pretty accurate insight into the mental activity and the creative urges expressed in the phantasy life. The direction and trends of the introversive tendencies give many useful hints. Pure mental creation finds expression in literary work, in scientific research and philosophy. Where there is a strong indication of manual dexterity in the *FC* factor, creative effort can take the form of art, of craftsmanship, engineering or similar constructive enterprises.

The extratensive personality of high intelligence without particular creative ability or urge will do better in a profession like law or medicine or the vocation of theology. If there is a richly gifted type with creative urge, art of a suitable kind offers a good outlet. Music appeals to the person with a strong emotional life and indifferent creative urge. One should be able to decide whether the person is a 'learner' and 'imitator' or a 'constructor and creator'. In this respect it is also helpful to examine the response series for special indications : is his approach synthetic or analytical? Does he remain on the outline of the blot, or does he penetrate into its interior?

All these points will help one to draw a conclusion about the type of work for which the patient is best fitted. Frequently one discovers latent talents and tendencies whose development had been neglected before, but which promise to be of sufficient importance to justify their cultivation. What is decisive in the end is the correlation of these factors with age, intelligence, and special circumstances.

# ELABORATION OF THE PERSONALITY PICTURE

A solid framework of the personality has now been constructed and into it one can proceed to fit the more subordinate responses which appear on the emotional side, the *FC'*, *C'F*, and *C'*, and the *Fc*, *cF* and *c* scores.

The former responses may appear merely as an enlargement of the emotional scale in a richly endowed personality which has produced a favourable assortment of colour responses. Their value in such a case is probably similar to that of the *FC*.

Where the *C'* responses are more numerous than the ordinary colour responses or replace them altogether, one speaks of a 'burnt child reaction', as it has been found that they are most commonly associated with infantile frustration of the emotional life. They express a guarded attitude towards emotional stirrings, a primary pessimism and distrust of these feelings. Such people are quite capable of unfolding under the influence of love and care. Theoretically at least, these pseudo-colour responses could be replaced by their colour equivalents, the *FC'* by *FC*, the *C'F* by *CF*, and the *C'* by *C*. Material is still lacking to show whether such a change actually ever does take place in real life. The variations of *C'* interpretations are less spontaneous than their *C* equivalents, and even the cruder forms do not seem to be linked with gross emotional instability.

The varieties of texture responses, *Fc* and *cF*, and *c* are still further removed from the colour scale, but they can be linked with it and judged in relation to it. The significance of sensuality in connection with the emotional life leads to a number of speculations which are worth considering. In small quantity and mainly form-linked these answers are a favourable sign of finer social perceptions. But if numerous, they suggest sensuality. It is therefore well to examine how these two different interpretations fit into the total personality. Where the test reveals a socially ill-adapted individual of low intelligence and inclination to crude emotional, as well as instinctive drives, one can hardly even in one *Fc* see the expression of finer feelings. Actual experience with clinical material amply justifies this view. The man of the labouring class who cannot resist the appeal of the opposite sex will frequently present such a picture in the record. On the other hand, one meets cases where a good many *c* responses of all types have been given, yet the clinical picture presents a person of fastidious tastes. Here the record will show a richly developed personality with a good intelligence and an equally good social adaptation who has his sensual dispositions as well as his emotional impulses well in hand. There is therefore a good deal of freedom allowable in the interpretation of these texture scores, a scope for the experience and ingenuity of the interpreter which makes the test the delicate instrument that it is.

# OTHER FACTORS FOR INTEGRATION INTO THE PERSONALITY PICTURE

Before proceeding to the investigation of the record for pathological features it is advisable to integrate some general observations into the picture so far obtained.

# The Assessment of the Personality

## THE PROBLEM OF THE TOTAL TIME TAKEN FOR THE RECORD, AND THE TOTAL NUMBER OF RESPONSES

It has already been mentioned that the majority of records average one response per minute, and that any gross deviation from this norm should receive attention. When the time exceeds this, there are a number of possible explanations, each of which must fit into the clinical aspect as well as the configuration of the personality. It may be due to the retardation associated with depressive states or it may be symptomatic of the impotent bewilderment accompanying many organic brain lesions. It is sometimes found in the more acute neurosis, and is common in the malingerer who does not want to commit himself by any spontaneous response, but carefully considers the possibilities and gives a banal answer after a long interval. Deliberate non-co-operation occasionally furnishes a similar picture, but here it is more common to find a time excess only for the first few cards and then an indifferent hurry to get the test finished as quickly as possible, since dilatory methods have failed to impress the tester. Or genuine interest has taken the place of the initial aversion for the task, and time is normal for the second half of the card series.

A shortening of the time is common in manics, hypo-manics, and allied conditions, as also in the logorrhoeic individual who wants to impress. Highly intelligent people also often show a better speed, but it must be remembered that to each card the first few responses may come fast enough, while the succeeding ones will take longer time till the initial gain has been exhausted.

## THE TURNING OF THE CARDS

The way in which the patient turns the cards for inspection is characteristic for each type and should not be overlooked. It does not require any degree of accuracy to arrive at an opinion and can be done easily from a few marks indicating the trend. But this trend is significant and must fit into the personality picture. It reflects interest, perplexity, distaste, impotence, furtiveness, dullness, aimless opportunism, or any other attitude one likes to identify with any one particular behaviour. It is most exceptional for a healthy intelligent person to look at the blot only in the position it was handed over. Should this happen, the suspicion arises that instructions were not fully understood. Mental defectives are usually loath to turn the cards.

111

## THE GENERAL ATTITUDE TOWARDS THE TEST

What has been said about the turning applies also to the general attitude of the patient. Co-operation and interest in the task are a great help, and where a record is qualitatively and quantitatively poor it is important to find whether the patient's general attitude can be blamed for this. Responses of spontaneity do not easily come from unwilling lips, and a hostile attitude will find expression in those monosyllabic answers that lack the simplest elaboration that would indicate a perception of movement or of colour.

Under the heading of general attitude fall also the analytic and the synthetic forms of approach. One wants to know whether the patient really understands the nature of the task or whether he is looking for 'cleverly hidden pictures' right up to Card X.

Expressions of pleasure or of disgust, of eagerness or of disappointment, of interest or of tiredness lend colour to the test result and help to assess it in its proper light.

# ABNORMAL FEATURES OF THE RECORD AND THEIR ASSESSMENT

Having obtained a primary outline of the personality, one can now proceed to look for abnormalities and to harmonize them with the basic personality till a solid clinical picture is obtained. By 'clinical picture' one understands a more comprehensive view of the person than is described in medical text-books. It embraces all abnormalities irrespective of whether they are giving rise to complaints or are being absorbed or sublimated in the daily existence. It is a good plan to go over the various danger points methodically in order not to miss anything of significance.

## THE PERSONALITY STRUCTURE

Here the most important factor which has not yet entered into the final assessment is the presence of $K$ or $k$. The former indicates, as previously explained, 'inner anxiety' and its significance is worst where it is isolated and strong. The aspect is more favourable if it is accompanied by $FK$ and perhaps $k$ as well, because this suggests that the patient is endeavouring to rationalize his anxiety and bring it under control.

Frequently a glance at the graph will show the likely cause of this inner anxiety: an inadequacy of $M$ in the presence of overwhelming numbers of $FM$ and $m$, particularly the latter, representing as it does the hostile inner forces, commonly leads to inner anxiety. If $M$ is poor, but $m$ absent, the emotional side may be responsible when there are predominantly $CF$ and $C$ responses. Sometimes one finds $K$ in a constricted graph as the only spontaneous response. The conjecture in such cases is that phantasy life as well as emotional reactions have been suppressed as disturbing factors and that the inner anxiety is the result of this process.

## THE CONTENT

Certain responses must be regarded as pathological, while others have this significance only when they are not the result of occupational interest. Among the former are those associated with crude $C$ like blood, or with $Cm$ like fire and explosions, and those connected with $K$: cloud or smoke. To the latter belong the customary responses. The significance of sexual responses must be assessed in each individual case; they are an indication of mental preoccupation rather than of any particular abnormality.

Pathological is colour naming, where the interpretation of the blot is avoided by merely naming its particular colour. This is frequently associated with organic brain lesions but occurs also in functional psychosis and in mental defectives. It is occasionally practised by neurotics. Artists may draw attention to their skill in giving certain shades a special name, but this should be classified as 'a comment on colour' since it seldom, if ever, replaces the real colour response. Where it does, one is justified in suspecting an abnormality in the personality. Form description should only occur in the first blot and this only as an initial failure to cope with the task set. It is of a higher mental quality than colour naming and suggests an inner disturbance by the chiaroscuro which prevents a logical interpretation of the shapes seen. The response has not the vagueness of a $K$ interpretation; it suggests a trend to 'empty formality', and is a response failure which may fit into a variety of personalities.

## THE CHARACTER OF THE RESPONSE

The occurrence of confabulatory responses, or of morbid or schizoid ones, their frequency and quality are next fitted into the Rorschach personality. Is confabulation associated with a sound intelligence and mature phantasy life or is it an escape from reality into a world of wishful thinking? Are the morbid responses connected with depression or anxiety, do they fit into a sadistic or masochistic picture? Are there any suspicions of homicidal or suicidal trends or are they the aftermath of some psychic trauma such as battle experience? How do schizoid responses tally with what has so far been discovered about the patient? Are they the product of an over-fertile imagination in an intelligent person of extensive reading or have they resulted from a split in the personality which no longer permits an accurate distinction between fact and fantasy? How bizarre and unnatural *are* the pictures visualized? Do they tally with the patient's previous or habitual content of phantasy or are they of recent origin? Are they associated with gross variations in the quality of the other responses, $F+$ being followed by a $F-$, or other signs of mental inadequacy or lability? When an uneducated labourer produces a number of prehistoric animals while inclined to score $F-$ a schizophrenic tendency is very likely, while a student of palaeontology ought not to produce $F-$ to any significant extent.

Responses in question form are an indication of uncertainty; it is the appeal for aid by asking to have an opinion supported or confirmed.

## REMARKS, EXCLAMATIONS AND REJECTIONS

Remarks should be examined individually and analysed as to their relevance. Their content may be suggestive or insignificant. They are most important where they reveal emotional reactions to colour or to darkness and can give useful hints about the reasons for subsequent responses and their correct interpretation.

Exclamations are assessed in a corresponding manner. Being of a more spontaneous character their significance is rather greater than that of the ordinary remark.

Rejections are always pathological. They are surprisingly often met with in the acute anxiety neuroses where the clinical picture frequently masks an incompetence of mental faculties. They are met with in such psychotic conditions where a mental failure is to be expected. A rejection therefore is of primary significance and affects the total personality picture adversely.

## THE PROPORTION $(A+H) : (Ad+Hd)$

Where this is equal or where the sum of details is greater than that of the whole figures one infers an inner uncertainty. A good deal of self-confidence is required to make out a total figure in a blot which only suggests a few parts of it. Those lacking confidence in their own judgment will prefer to stick to the detail of a figure—human or animal—which to their eye seems unequivocal. They are afraid of incurring criticism by venturing further afield, are not quite certain whether they are 'piecing the things together in the right way', and desist from trying to identify a whole figure when they find some parts missing.

The significance of this formula is similar to that of the question response, but the two do not very frequently appear together in the same record. In the latter case it is an appeal to the outer world for support, in the former it is an inner denial of strength which the patient tries to keep hidden.

## SPECIAL FORMULAE FOR DIAGNOSTIC PURPOSES

In the course of experience with the test the association of certain features with particular clinical pictures has become recognized and an attempt has been made to group them for the purpose of diagnosis. It is an enterprise fraught with danger to the unwary, for nothing defeats the purpose of the test more readily than cut-and-dried formulae which tend to remove it from the sphere of individual judgment and the experience that the worker has gained in the realm of psychiatry. The inner significance of the method must be understood, or even the most promising formulae will only lead to gross errors in diagnosis.

If certain well-known ones are given here, it is with the understanding that they are not to be blindly accepted as diagnostic labels, but to be used as aids towards a further insight into the personality in the hope of obtaining a clear picture. Where they give a positive answer they are of greatest importance, but where they fail it does not of necessity mean that the complex in question is non-existent. A great many gross hysterics fail to give the 'signs of hysteria', and some of the most typical neurotics do not give enough 'signs of neurosis' for a positive diagnosis by the formula alone.

## SIGNS OF SHOCK[1]

In his original work Rorschach believed that the neurotic would betray his emotional reaction to colour by a perceptible hesitation

[1] Brosin, H. W. and Fromm, E. O.: 'Rorschach and Colour Blindness.' *Ror. Reg. Esch.*, Vol. IV, April 1940, pp. 39–70.

leading to a lengthening of the response time. This does doubtless occur in some cases, but in others there is either no difference or the balance is in favour of an even faster reaction time for the coloured cards. This 'colour shock' is therefore not a reliable sign. 'Shading shock' has been claimed as a sign of neurosis on the same ground; undoubtedly there are patients who dislike the sombre grounds of darkness and hesitate to respond. But this reaction is by no means characteristic of the neuroses only.

Finally the various ways in which colour shock can find expression were tabulated, and the following observations selected as significant:

### Delay in the Reaction Time

This should be particularly noticeable when Cards II and VIII respectively are handed to the patient. The time taken for the first response should significantly exceed the average time for the first responses to the monochrome blots. Sometimes the average reaction time to all the coloured cards is longer than that to the grey ones.

### Number of Responses lowered for the Coloured Cards

This is again specially significant in relation to Cards II and VIII.

### The Quality of the Responses is Lowered

$F-$ appears in the coloured cards or there is a failure of $M$ when elsewhere movement responses are freely given.

### The Content is Poorer

The $A$ percentage for the coloured cards has risen, or there are too many stereotyped interpretations.

### Failure to Produce 'Popular' Responses to the Coloured Cards

In particular is such a reaction suggested when the human-like figures in Card III escape detection or the 'animal' (lateral red) in Card VIII has not been spotted.

### The Order is Disturbed

This very seldom happens as a result of 'colour shock'. Theoretically, the order $W-D-d$ is supposed to be abandoned under the influence of this 'shock', but where the succession is clearly marked it is the scattering of the total pattern rather than the colour that induces the patient to change his methods. Many neurotics give a

*W* to Card II as the first response, but can't think of a satisfactory whole-blot interpretation to III and X any more than many healthy people can.

## Rejections

These are always significant, and are so common in neurotics that it is of little importance whether they occur in respect to coloured blots or monochromes. Rejections of Cards II and VIII are far less frequent than of Cards IV and VII.

## Exclamations

These very often betray an emotional reaction to colour. They are a subordinated part of colour shock and neither regular in their appearance, nor exclusively due to mental tension.

## Comment on Colour

The patient gains time by making a few remarks about the colour before responding, or else gives expression to his views on the colours later on in his series of responses to the coloured card. It is more often a sign of sensitivity to colour schemes than of a definite 'shock', but such personalities are frequently found among the neurotics.

## Colour Shyness

There are responses to the black parts of Blots II and III, but the red has been left severely alone. This applies especially to Card II. In view of the frequency with which the neurotic identifies those red patches with 'blood' this is not surprising. Another form of colour shyness is the avoidance of aggressive and bright colours, specially the reds and yellows, and a preference for interpretations of green and blue blots.

When any of these factors have been traced in the record it is essential that one has convincing evidence that they are due to the influence of colour and not to the general pattern. One or two unequivocal signs are of greater value than 7–8 dubious ones. Card II is probably of greater significance than the subsequent coloured ones, and should therefore receive particular attention. For diagnostic purposes, however, the whole problem of 'colour shock' plays a subordinated role. 'Shading shock' is assessed on similar lines, but as it does not occur without more important abnormalities in the record it is of even less importance and need not trouble the beginner.

117

## SIGNS OF NEUROSIS

The experience with acute war neuroses suggests an enlargement of the list of factors in order to bring it up to date. This addition will be pointed out, otherwise the scheme is that suggested by Miale and Harrower Erickson.[1]

### Total Responses less than Twenty-five

The intelligent adult neurotic will, however, frequently exceed a hundred.

### Rejection

This must be accepted *eo ipso* as a pathological reaction.

### Colour Shock

Any positive indication of this type can now be ranged here among the neurotic traits of the record.

### Alternately, Shading Shock

This is, however, such an uncertain quantity that it is suggested it be replaced by the incidence of a $K$ response, since this expresses 'inner anxiety'.

### FC Responses

Less than two.

### M Responses

Less than two.

### FM Responses

More numerous than $M$ responses.

### F

Exceeding 50 per cent.

### A

Exceeding 50 per cent.

### Suggestive Content of Responses

Anatomy, blood, fire, and allied responses unless occupationally

[1] F. R. Miale, B.S., and M. R. Harrower Erickson, PH.D.: 'Personality Structure in the Psychoneuroses.' *Ror. Res. Exch.*, April 1940, pp. 71–4.

justified. (This, like $K$ previously mentioned, is an addition to the scheme.) It is very rare to find all these signs present in a record, and seven out of ten constitute a positive result. More often only five or six of the factors will be elicited in cases which are clinically undoubtedly neuroses. Acute cases conform more readily with the scheme than the chronics, and the degree of severity seems to produce a similar tendency.

The scheme is likely to fail where the responses are very numerous, because there are seldom any rejections in these cases, and $M$ responses though percentually low occur more often than twice. The $A$ percentage also cannot be relied upon, for it is usually between 40 and 50 per cent and the signs of colour shock are found to be ambiguous. In such instances the answer must come from the other factors, viz. $FC$ less than two, $FM$ more numerous than $M$, $F$ exceeding 50 per cent, and some abnormality of content or else a $K$ response. If these four signs are present the odds are heavily in favour of a neurosis.

## HERTZ' SIGNS OF HYSTERIA

For a thorough understanding of this formula the reader is recommended to study Hertz' publications on hysteria. (See Rapaport, D: Diagnostic Psychol. Testing, Vol. II, pp. 85–394; The Year Book Publishers Inc., Chicago, 1946). It is specially valuable for children and adolescents, but signs are often absent in cases of gross motor or sensory hysteria.

While the anxiety neurotic tends to restrict his spontaneity by an outward show of control of emotion and thus produces a constricted picture with a high $F$ percentage and relatively few other responses, the hysteric abandons himself to his impulses. $F$ percentage is low—usually below 40 per cent—and the graph shows a dilated picture in which a wide range of different spontaneous responses is displayed. Typical of the hysteric is his lack of control over his emotional reactions and his inability to make the necessary social adaptation. $CF$ is therefore represented in greater numbers than $FC$, and 1–2 $C$ are usually found as well. The sum of the colour responses exceeds the number of $M$'s, and the latter are fewer than the $FM$ responses. Inanimate movement, $m$, is also commonly present. About 50 per cent of hysterics conform with this picture; it frequently fails to appear in cases of conversion hysteria, where the clinical diagnosis is unequivocal, while the hysterical predisposition and temperament

119

commonly reveal it. Here, again, the Rorschach record reflects the personality with its potentialities and changes, rather than a particular clinical manifestation.

## PIOTROWSKI'S SIGNS OF ORGANIC LESION

These are of considerable value because they express some essential features of the condition at an early stage, often before the clinical picture has become clear. The record is usually small, and the responses seldom exceed fifteen in number. The total time taken is abnormally long, and 20–30 minutes are often needed to obtain those few responses. This is largely due to an attitude of impotence and of perplexity; impotence, because the patient realizes the poverty of his response but is incapable of improving or of withdrawing it, and perplexity, because he realizes his difficulties and inadequacies, doubts his own judgment, and turns to the examiner for reassurance. Question form of response is common. There is frequently perseveration of ideas, the patient repeating a previous response automatically although it does not fit the blot or repetition of the same idea with or without variations. $F-$ scores reach a relatively high percentage, Human movement is always below two in number, and colour naming should occur at least once, while Popular responses are usually abnormally low, being replaced by Originals of poor quality. Five to six of these signs are usually present together.[1]

Piotrowski points out that organic cases are unable to synthetize many details into one good interpretation; they are poor in distinguishing essential parts from those of secondary importance. They believe that the blots represent definite objects which they must recognize. Their associations are poor and uniform; phraseologies are frequently repeated. Approach and succession are usually normal, co-operation is mostly good and the patient is interested in his achievement. There is a diminution of the introversive part of the personality with increase of extratensive elements: the patient tends to become a self-centred extravert.

All these formulae express the dominant tendencies of each clinical group. It is the atypical case that will fail to conform, a circumstance particularly well illustrated by the organic lesions of the central nervous system with their variety of syndromes. The various factors are the ones most frequently found in the records given in these patho-

[1] Piotrowski, Z. A.: 'Organic Lesions.' *Ror. Res. Exch.*, Vol. I, No. 2, Nov. 1936, pp. 23–39.

logical conditions. It cannot be stressed too often that there is no single type of response that is in itself of diagnostic significance, but that it is always the combination of many factors. Only when this is constantly kept in mind can these groups of diagnostic signs render reliable assistance, and the danger of turning first to them for guidance is to be avoided.

## THE ANALYSIS OF THE CONTENT

It is less misleading to attempt an analysis of the response series after a personality configuration has been elaborated, than to start with it. Analysis of the answers the patient has given to the blots is so largely based on intuition and conjecture, so open to misinterpretation, that it should be guided by the more solid and reliable data obtained from the score sheet. Frequently by the time one has settled down to the record one has forgotten the patient's humour, the inflection of his voice or some extraneous circumstance which influenced a notable response. All this becomes less important when there is already a personality picture to guide the content analysis and into which to fit the result.

It would lead too far if an attempt were made to discuss all the possible problems. Here just a few of the more common points of interest will be mentioned.

In the first place the form of the response furnishes a useful information. Does the patient show a marked preference for a certain formula, such as 'This reminds me of . . .' or 'That is like . . .' or 'I can see a . . .' or 'There is . . .'? Does he stick to it right to the end or does he gradually or suddenly change to another one? Are there grammatical idiosyncrasies?

Then one is always interested in subjects that figure repeatedly among the content. Are they due to poverty of ideas and merely repetitions due to inadequacy? Have they a special significance in the patient's life and, if so, is there a deeper psychological one hidden behind them? Is the interest rational and natural, or incongruous? It has been said that a feeling of affinity with the rest of humanity stands in relationship to the number of *H* and *Hd* responses; does an excess of responses drawn from e.g. the vegetable kingdom suggest a vegetative attitude of mind, a sort of cabbage personality? Are there many weapons among the objects, or sharp or pointed instruments? Could they have a symbolic meaning? Do they occur particularly in areas of blot which suggest sexual parts? Or is it a case of 'war nerves' and apprehension of battle stress? Could there be suicidal or homicidal tendencies?

Do the responses suggest a keen intelligence or the average level, and does this impression tally with the estimate of the I.Q.? Has any attempt been made to give the interpretations an intellectual air, by the use of pretentious phraseology or pseudo-scientific or philosophical commentary?

Has he grasped the nature of the blots or does he persist to the end in pointing out the inevitable symmetries and repetitions? Is he fond of enumerating his discoveries in the way sometimes practised by children?

These are a few of the commoner problems, and should serve to illustrate the aim of the content analysis and its scope. Occasionally there is useful evidence of free association which is suitable for further discussion with the patient, but more commonly the responses are of the nature of a screen memory and do not lend themselves to deeper analysis.

With this survey of the content the test record has furnished all the essential information it contains, and a short summary of the significant findings should enable one to arrive at a diagnosis, when such is the aim, or at vocational or other advice, if that is sought.

# 6

## SOME USEFUL ELABORATIONS
## OF THE TEST

These concern mainly the scoring of unusual responses and their interpretation. In this additional chapter an attempt has been made to help the beginner over those difficulties everyone finds himself up against sooner or later, when the scoring seems to be inadequate to do justice to the occasion.

### ADDITIONS TO THE 'MENTAL APPROACH'

The $W$ responses play an important role in the test, and their quality enters into the assessment of the intellectual level. It happens sometimes that a $W$ response is inspired by a small detail of the blot, which is appropriately interpreted in itself but the total object does not fit the whole blot satisfactorily. If $F-$ were scored in such cases this would probably be too severe, since some accurate identification has occurred. For such instances the symbol

$$Wv$$

was suggested, the '$v$' being based on the German word '$vulgär$', meaning 'ordinary' or what is colloquially termed 'cheap'. The patient has discovered a cheap way of arriving at a $W$ response. The two small claw-like projections at the top of Blot I or the equally claw-like ends of the detached lower 'legs' of Blot III sometimes induce the $Wv$ response of 'crab'. The fringed top of Card VI is suggestive of a winged creature, and the whole blot called an insect. Card X being composed of many shapes which are reminiscent of animals, the whole is indiscriminately interpreted as 'a medley of all sorts of animals': *Wv*. A more critical faculty is expressed in such qualifying additions as 'Walt Disney cartoon', or 'A memory of D.T.'s' and when the colour factor in this card has also been taken into consideration, as in the not uncommon 'marine landscape', the response is above the level of the ordinary *Wv* and scores a *W*.

The *Wv* is scored where a minor detail has been correctly interpreted but should not have been extended to a whole blot. (*Pars pro toto* response.)

## THE MENTAL APPROACH AND BECK'S 'ORGANIZING TALENT' *Z*[1]

Beck recognized very rightly some years ago that a significance must be attached to the knack shown by some people of organizing scattered parts of blot into a uniform picture. His original scheme is well worth studying and is found in his 'Introduction'.[2] He devised a method of giving different values to different combinations of distant parts of a blot or combination with white spaces. He assessed the relative merits of the *W* responses to the various cards and standardized all the significant factors.

Here a slight modification of Beck's method will be discussed, some alterations having been suggested by the work done in co-operation with Personnel Selection in the Army. In the first place it was found that a high percentage of *W* scores *per se* would suggest an organizing talent that was not present in the man in actual fact. Certainly for military purposes more was required than the ability to make a patchwork quilt from odds and ends. Only three cards require an outstanding ability for the production of a qualitatively good *W*: Cards III, IX and X. Blot II is perhaps the threshold of such an ability, and an average organizing talent should be able to produce a *W* to it. If this does not occur the suspicion arises that there is some colour shock, when elsewhere the *W* trend is normal. For selection purposes an emotionally unstable organizer cannot be recommended, and *W* failure to Blot II always demands a careful

[1] Beck, S. J.: *Introduction to the Rorschach Method: A Manual of Personality Study.*
[2] See p. 7.

analysis of the personality picture in such cases. But where II has produced its *W* response, it is worth while looking for further indications.

In the first place combinations of the whole blot with the white spaces can be scored as

$$WS$$

in the Mental Approach column to facilitate a quick survey. The finding of such scores in the Approach Column will at once draw attention to them and their likely significance. It is doubtful however whether the 'map of an island all surrounded by sea' is of any value. Possibly only when elaborated with 'inland lakes' and further detail.

Secondly, all combinations of white space with detail. They are scored as *DS* or *dS* underneath the *S*, as unusual responses belonging to the *dd+S* group.

And finally the 'rare detail' responses, the *Dr* of the earlier authors. These should approximate the size of a major detail, but be composed of parts which do not lie in close apposition. Blots IX and X produce the most examples of such a capacity for organizing the separated pieces into a linked unit.

A definite correlation between these Rorschach factors and mental or practical organizing ability has been found, but their real significance appears only within the total personality picture, in particular in connection with the predominance of introversive or extratensive traits and intellectual level.

The final picture must serve to specify what kind of an organizer the patient is or is likely to be. This 'organizing talent' is an interesting speculation which occasionally produces useful results. But there are many people with considerable gifts in that direction whose *Z* factor is not in the least suggestive. In those cases the analysis of Approach and Succession is a more reliable indication.

# ENLARGEMENTS OF THE PERSONALITY STRUCTURE

### *Mm* RESPONSES

Here the more accurate definition of the movement responses, viz. the scoring of 'expressive poses', must find room. As these should be rated lower than the fully active *M*, the symbol

$$Mm$$

indicating its immaturity is suggested.

It would go too far to adopt the same critical attitude towards *FM* as well, although there are occasionally records collected where birds have spread their wings without flying, dogs lie stretched in front of the hearth, or cows ruminate in the meadow. To reduce the significance of these animal poses would lessen the relative weight of *FM* in the *FM* : *M* balance, and would give the impression of a maturer personality than is actually the case. So far clinical experience has furnished no evidence that finer shadings of animal movement require distinction. The evidence is rather in favour of scoring animal poses that do not include at least some form of motion, as *F*, and to start from such attitudes as 'crouching', 'going to spring', 'sniffing', which at least contain the elements of a movement phantasy.

With the human movement responses the case is different, because one tries to assess the maturity and power of phantasy life and mental capacity, and because those immature forms do appear so often in childhood as precursors of the real *M*.

When a record is lengthy it saves a good deal of time to find significant features attached to the scoring in the tabulation, where they attract attention. This is particularly to the point in the case of *M*, which figures both quantitatively and qualitatively. It is therefore good practice to score outstandingly good human movement with *M*+; the view has already been given expression that *M* − is very difficult to assess. On the other hand the *dddM* combinations are worthy of record on the tabulation sheet. In this way one is enabled to get a clear picture of the qualities of the *M* responses at a glance.

## THE COMBINATIONS OF *m* WITH *K* OR *C*

Examples are 'running water' (*Km*) and 'spurting blood' (*Cm*). These *Km* and *Cm* scores are very useful because they show the close connection between the instinctive or hostile inner forces and inner anxiety or powerful emotional reactions. The more advanced worker will therefore give such responses his particular attention. On the tabulation *Km* is commonly scored between *m* and *K*, preferably on the *K* side, since this factor is usually the dominant. *Cm* contains an element of form and ranges itself preferably between *CF* and *C*.

## DIFFICULT FORMS OF *K*, AND COMBINATIONS

Some chiaroscuro responses lack the shapelessness of pure *K*, but fall neither into the *k* nor the *FK* class. To these belong 'dark trees',

# Some Useful Elaborations of the Test

'landscape by night' (without a perspective element), and similar responses which lay stress on the abstract or literal suggestion of darkness. An ominous atmosphere sensed in the chiaroscuro is so obviously connected with inner anxiety that a $K$ combination is the only correct score, e.g. $KF$.

Occasionally a response seems to have its origin in the contrast between light and dark, and the white ground is treated as 'light', while the actual blot is disposed of as a more or less shapeless mass. Clinically there seems to exist a relationship with the anxiety states, but so far the evidence is inconclusive. Such unusual responses should, however, be scored in a special way not only to attract attention but also to prevent their being scored in the wrong place. Analogous to Earl's ingenious form-colour combinations which will be discussed presently, the symbols

$$K/F \text{ and } F/K$$

are suggested. A 'look at the sky from the inside of a cave' (Card II), for instance, would be $K/F$, while a 'house with the windows lit up' (Card I), or a 'bombed building with the sky through the windows' would be $F/K$. In the one case the $K$ factor appears to dominate, in the other form perception.

## EARL'S $F/C$ AND $C/F$ RESPONSES[1]

Sometimes a response contains neither an interpretation of form nor of colour. An example is the impressionistic 'Walt Disney cartoon' answer to Card X unless elaborated further. The vivid colouring is reminiscent of those cartoons on general grounds, yet the separation of the blots and their clear-cut shapes add strongly to the impression. Yet neither the colours nor the forms have been interpreted, and the response is neither a $CF$ nor a $C$.

Another frequent response is that of 'coloured map', most commonly given to IX. Neither form nor colour have been interpreted yet neither have they been ignored. For such responses Earl created the symbols

$$F/C \text{ and } C/F$$

covering the range from the predominance of the form factor in the response to that of colour.

These are emotional responses to the *variety* of colours and shapes. Their significance in the test picture is similar to that of the $CF$.

[1] Earl, C. J. C.: 'A Note on the validity of certain Rorschach Symbols.' *Ror. Res. Exch.*, Vol. V, No. 2, April 1941, pp. 51–61.

## COLOUR INTERPRETED SYMBOLICALLY, *C symb.*

This is also an impressionistic response, but instead of finding a material simile an abstract one is produced. It also differs from the previous response in that individual colours are selected. For instance, the blue blots 'suggest cool reason', 'the red is like a life force', 'the green reminds me of hope and faith', 'the yellow patches look like jealousy'. These are abstractions of the pure *C* response and obviously indicate a higher level of emotional life than the ordinary *C*, an attempt to identify emotional influences, if not to control them. Where they appear in company with *C* answers, the suspicion arises that they are merely a modification, an attempt at rationalization of emotions. Where they are the only form of *C*, their emotional value is the same as that of *CF*. These *C symb.* should be analysed and interpreted individually at the end of the assessment. From an artistic or a literary personality they seem to come naturally, while in an untalented person they suggest schizoid trends.

Klopfer[1] characterizes it as a pure colour response with a tabulation value of 1·5, though psychologically belonging to *CF*, since 'the impact is mitigated by some rational element'. While colour description is given predominantly by artistic subjects, colour symbolism is frequently the response of those 'at odds with their own strong inclination to react to emotional stimuli from without'.

## COMBINATIONS OF *C* WITH *c* OR *K*

Where it is evident that the response is based not on colour only but on a discrimination of texture or to finer variations of shading, this fact must be recorded. Where it is considered that the colour has first attracted attention and acted as a sort of gate-opener, the response is scored between *CF* and *C*.

The *C* or *K* factor should never be ignored, because it is unusual for a pure *C* response to take cognizance of anything but crude colour. It lies in the very nature of the emotional reaction that the power of observation is impaired. The pink cloud or the green wool are modifications of the *C* response, the one in the direction of anxiety, the other towards sensual perception. There is reason to believe that their combination modifies the significance of the factors involved and one is therefore doing greater justice to the personality which is

[1] Klopfer (*Ror. Res. Exch.*, Vol. III, No. 4, August 1939, pp. 164 and 189).

# Some Useful Elaborations of the Test

being tested by the combined scoring, placed among the colour responses unless there are strong indications to the contrary.

## THE POSITION RESPONSE, *Po*

This was introduced by Beck (see Beck's *Introduction*)[1] as a pathological response not due to shape, colour or tone of the blot detail in question, but to its position relative to another part of the blot. There are two types which are not uncommon: the 'Geographical' and the 'Abstract' *Po*. The former produces such replies as 'This line down the middle could be the axis of the world' to the centre line in Card I, or, referring to the 'boot' of Blot IV. 'This could be the West of England', and after a while a small spot inside the upper part of the blot is pointed to 'This could be Edinburgh'. Of the latter kind are responses like this one to Card IX: 'It suggests the breaking away of two worlds—a good one is splitting itself off from a bad one, and they are in flames', and later the thin orange line linking the tops is scrutinized: 'This is the spiritual link that cannot be broken.' Or to Card X 'There is a fight going on up here (lateral blue). Those blue forces are hard pressed.' Later, referring to the orange-brown blots, lower lateral quadrant: 'These two might possibly be made use of to hang on to by the blues—as a reserve.'

The first example belongs to the record of a man of low intelligence who rejected or repressed the idea of 'map of the world' to the whole blot, but who continued his initial trend of thought till the central line inspired him to the 'axis' response.

The others are really the additional responses which elaborate a previous concept. The patient is creating relationships between distant details, harmonizing them into *Dr* responses. Where these elaborations gradually amount to a *W* interpretation, there can no longer be any question of a *Po* score, since all parts are judged in relation to each other in this case. The important factors are the selection of a new detail of the blot for interpretation, the failure of the orthodox methods for doing so, and the solution of the problem by linking it ideologically with another, separated part of the blot.

The *Po* response is not peculiar to any level of intelligence or any particular clinical picture. It is unusual and unorthodox, and should therefore be examined for its possible significance in relation to the total personality. In each case it should be decided which is its most significant feature: the particular choice of detail, the escape from

[1] See p. 7.

I          129

the usual methods of responding, the content, or the confabulatory, morbid or schizoid character of the content.

## ADDITIONS TO THE CONTENT

### THE *Hdx* AND *Adx* RESPONSES

Rorschach discovered the predilection some mental defectives show for minute details which could be interpreted as 'fingers', 'toes', 'noses', or any other small part of the body. He called them '*Oligophrene Kleindetails*' in the belief that they were due to mental deficiency. It was subsequently found that they occurred in a variety of different conditions and that the constant characteristic was not so much the choice of a minute part of the blot, as the tendency to see only a small member of a human or animal body where usually a complete head or a total figure would be identified.

The *x* responses represent a failure to raise a sub-conscious perception to a conscious level. The patient has looked at a certain part of the blot, conceived the picture of a figure on a sub-conscious level and becomes only aware of a fragment of this conception. 'Two hands clapped together', referring to the upper medial spearpoint in Card II is all that is consciously recognized of the two figures represented by the whole blot. 'A nose' is the only response to the human-like shapes in Card III, singling out the pointed inner end of the upper extremity of the black blot. Similar 'noses' may be spotted along the upper edge of the bat's wing in V or the outer edge of the green in IX, both commonly described as complete profiles. In IV only the 'eyes' of the lower head-like shape may be elicited, or 'a hand hanging down' as a response to the upper lateral, snake-like excrescence, or the 'toes' of the boot-like lower lateral shape be described without taking cognizance of the main detail.

In VI the two tiny straight lines on either side of the upper end of the blot produce 'whiskers', a response which could only have arisen out of the sub-conscious recognition of a 'head' to which these lines are attached. In VIII one of the 'legs' of the lateral pink animal is identified, while the most common of all responses is not made. In Card IX the eye or the antlers of the stag's head in the medial portion of the green are spotted without any recognition of the rest, and of the 'popular' pink face only the 'moustache' is detected. The green rabbit's head in the lower central portion of X is not identified, but the 'rabbit's ears' are mentioned. Perhaps the 'finger' or 'pointing finger' seen in the lower inner end of the detached limb of the black portion of Card III also belongs here.

These are examples of *Hdx* and *Adx* responses which are not uncommon.

They should not include those that are based upon deliberate evasion out of shyness or prudery, as in the case of the central figure in Blot I, suggestively feminine, which may induce the patient to respond only to the lowest tip with a furtive 'somebody's feet'. Such escapist tactics should be assessed under the heading of sexual responses and attitude to sex.

These *x* responses may arise either from the presence of a powerful repression or from a defective intelligence which does not allow the patient to grasp common concepts to their full extent. They are frequently met with in organic brain lesions and in mental defect, but are also not uncommon in hysterics and schizophrenics, and can sometimes be associated with other conditions.

## ADDITIONAL RELATIONSHIPS

Some workers put forward the suggestion that the relationship

$$(FM+m) : (\text{total } c + \text{total } C')$$

should be studied.

So far it does not appear to have contributed materially to the personality picture. *FM* and *m* are the least controlled and most primitive inner urges, while surface texture and black-white responses are a higher order of perception. Furthermore, *c* responses cannot be mechanically added to *C'* ones which express a different type of extratensive reaction. To speculate upon the significance of crude *c* or crude *C'* in relationship to *FM* and *m*, however, seems justifiable. The implication raised by pure *c* in the presence of more $(FM+m)$ than *M*, is that it is primitive sensuality which must arouse equally primitive instincts. In the case of *C'* the emotional repressions of the 'burnt child' activate infantile or immature phantasy pictures and desires, not necessarily of a sensual nature.

More important is the problem of inner anxiety in relation to the primitive instincts: $(m+FM) : (\text{total } K+k+FK)$. Here we find a possible answer to the question: what happens to those primitive instincts in the absence of adequate mature phantasy? How much of it is extruded, and how much is converted into anxiety? This relationship is based on clinical experience, for it is well known that an excess of $m$ can produce inner anxiety. It is not advisable to convert $(K+k+FK)$ into a total sum in the way the colour responses are added up for comparison with $M$. Both the $(m+FM)$ and the $(K+k+FK)$ are on the introversive side of the balance, and we know as yet very little about a person's capacity for converting primitive impulses into anxiety on a quantitative basis. The various factors should therefore be compared in the light of their respective significance and a tentative conclusion drawn, which must then fit into the basic personality.

Another relationship of interest is that of

$$(K+k+FK) : (\text{total } c+\text{total } C')$$

Here it is justifiable to add the various types of $c$ and $C'$ responses together, because the $K$ responses also vary in form control, and the aim is to discover how the introversive chiaroscuro responses balance the extratensive ones and vice versa.

The laws of these relationships are as yet largely based on conjecture. Rich personalities seldom give introversive shading responses without producing some also on the extratensive side. Interpretations of shading are given by persons who are sensitive, and this sensitivity varies in quality from crude to fine on the introversive as well as on the extratensive side. A study of these relationships is well worth while in cases where the record furnishes a good number and variety of chiaroscuro responses.

# 7

## SOME DIAGNOSTIC ADDENDA

Bearing in mind that everybody has a breaking-point at which the inner strain combined with the outer circumstances will deprive him of the free use of some of his faculties, it will be understood that the variety of personality picture is almost unlimited when the clinical material is examined. But one can trace predominant features and common patterns which, superimposed on the basic personality, betray the nature of the condition from which the person is suffering.

Many excellent personalities have finally broken down under extreme and prolonged battle stress, while many predisposed ones have walked along the borderline of a breakdown throughout their sheltered existence without coming to grief. The former have become battle casualties with a relatively favourable Rorschach record, while the latter are still leading useful lives although on paper they are in a worse condition.

If this reasoning is reversed, one finds that the test result furnishes the prognosis, gives the probabilities and shows the fundamental constitution.

## THE 'NORMAL' PERSONALITY IN FACT AND IN RECORD

Psychological 'normality' is a concept of relativity signifying that an individual is capable of utilizing all his faculties and fulfilling all his natural functions, in perfect harmony with himself and his fellow-men, leading an independent existence while fitting perfectly into human society, according to his particular sex, age, race and social group.

The standards of 'normality' in the Rorschach scheme are based on tendencies, reactions and capacities, while in practical life the dominant factor is behaviour. The value of the method depends upon the accuracy with which behaviour can be predicted and defined. This is only possible within the limits of the group to which that particular person belongs, and one is therefore confronted with a series of personality pictures which differ widely in scope and character, yet can all claim to represent a 'normal' configuration for the group in question.

A personality will be the more complex and rich the greater the sum of his intelligence and experience. The Rorschach method will therefore reveal a series of pictures of varying complexity according to the potentialities and the development of each individual.

To decide whether a personality should be considered 'normal' or otherwise it must be remembered that one single abnormal feature may be of significance in a simple and small record, while in an expansive one, several may appear without upsetting the balance of the personality to any great extent. The more intricate problems and experiences of life are frequently ignored by the person of low intelligence; but if they should intrude themselves into consciousness, they are apt to cause symptoms because they cannot be dealt with adequately by his mental faculties. A person of high intelligence has greater gifts for observation and for abstraction and therefore tries to assimilate experiences. The results of this process of assimilation are diverted into various channels, and it would be astounding if these riches could all be stored without causing some friction here or there. Even the highest intelligence can only aspire to a fragmentary knowledge, and some problems of existence may give rise to mild inner anxiety or lead to other reactions of inadequacy.

It is therefore not difficult to classify a personality of simple make-up as 'normal' because gross or significant indications of abnormality are lacking. But with a highly endowed and developed one it requires considerable judgment to assess the extent to which unusual responses and other factors may affect the total harmony of the 'Gestalt'. The vital aim of existence is to harness all inner and outer experiences as driving powers for further development of the personality and for achievement. The primitive instincts, the passionate depth of emotion, sensuality and anxiety, can all be sublimated and utilized for higher aims, and forced to undergo evolutionary changes in their qualitative aspect. The object of the test is to determine the chances of such a sublimatory process taking place in a superior personality, taking also into consideration the outer circumstances, which may be helpful or frustrating.

In practical life the criterion of 'normality' is behaviour. If the configuration of the Rorschach record suggests that that person will respond with normal behaviour to the ordinary circumstances of the environment into which he belongs, he can be regarded as 'normal'.

## THE NEUROSES

These have already received attention in the chapter on the final assessment of the personality. What has been said about the 'normals' also applies here. One sign of gross neurotic predisposition in the framework of a simple personality is far more suggestive than when the same occurs in a rich one. Each type of neurosis has its predominant feature, although they frequently have other features in common.

The obsessional states are not easily identified; many can be visualized as an escape from an inner conflict on lines parallel to those which govern conversion hysteria, the latter representing flight into a belief, the former into behaviour. Frequently anxiety can be traced in the early stages, and the introversive-extratensive balance may reveal the ruminative or the impulsive trends. The middle-aged obsessional often shows his unfavourable prognosis in depressive features that can no longer be rationalized. Apart from such outer characteristics of the record as would naturally suggest an obsessional disposition—e.g. rigid order of succession, regular turning, attention to the number of responses given to each card, remarks about symmetry and recurrent shapes—there is a tendency to search the inner area of the blot, and $k$ responses are common.

## THE PSYCHOSES

Enough has been said about the few points which are commonly associated with schizophrenic records to enable a diagnosis to be made in conjunction with the clinical picture. Search is made for a reflection of the schism in the personality, for the incongruity that marks the condition. That this is most commonly marked in the $F+ : F-$ and the character of the content, is incidental.

The depressive states give rise to a number of features which may appear singly or in groups. The withdrawal into phantasy with a high movement response ratio is more characteristic of the manic-depressive type with clearly defined phases than of melancholia. In the latter and in the reactive depressions the chiaroscuro responses of the anxiety type are numerous, $F$ percentage is high, and spontaneity correspondingly reduced. The time factor is usually increased in all types. The content reveals often a morbid or macabre trend of mind, and there may be a pronounced poverty of ideas.

Paranoia, especially in the early stages, does not seem to give rise to a uniform or characteristic picture as an entity, but individual records should leave little doubt; frequently the correct diagnosis is reached by a process of elimination of the possibility of another form of psychosis.

*For the Organic Reaction Types* see Piotrowski's formula and comment.

## MENTAL DEFECT

The significant factors relating to this condition have been discussed under the heading of assessment of the intellectual level. Apart from identifying peculiarities of various mental age levels in the record, e.g. the appearance of human movement responses or the form of the approach, the lower grades of defect furnish many bizarre responses. Repetitions and perseverations are common, chiaroscuro responses not rare. *Po* and *x* answers are also a frequent occurrence. The general lack of inner and outer control is expressed in the crude *C* or *m* and *FM* responses.

## OTHER CONDITIONS
### EPILEPSY

It would be a great boon if this condition could be diagnosed at an early stage from the Rorschach record, but this is not the case, all optimistic publications on the subject to the contrary. Once the state of mental deterioration has set in the picture becomes more characteristic. But by that time the findings of the test are only of academic interest. There are no 'epileptic' signs that are not common to other conditions as well, and individual records show the greatest diversity of configuration. The most significant feature is found in the basic personality where the picture points to emotional instability and lack of inner control, a strong indication that the individual may behave in an unreasonable manner under emotional stress, possibly in the form of fits or temper tantrums. The majority of cases are strongly extratensive, but the configuraions vary. The question which the record has to answer is whether that particular personality is likely to express loss of self-control in the form of fits.

## ENURESIS

Relatively few cases of enuresis have an organic basis and the spina bifida occulta is so rare that it does not affect the view that the complaint is essentially of functional origin. The Rorschach personalities are therefore as diverse as the causes of the trouble. But it is commonly associated with inner anxiety and a concern about health expressed in $K$ and Anatomy responses, both logical concomitants of the condition. The average intelligence of the enuretic is high, and there is usually a marked difference between the inadequately trained dullard and the neurotic reactive enuretic. The latter group, excluding the dullards, averages an I.Q. several per cent above that of the average population.

## JUVENILE DELINQUENCY

There are too many causes of delinquency for one ever to hope to establish a typical picture in the Rorschach record. Occasionally, however, one comes across a pattern that becomes familiar in time: a combination of $M$, $FC$ and $ddd$ responses. It is the type of child who has a good intelligence, a vivid phantasy life, and a physical taste for agility, but whose outer circumstances offer no opportunity for an outlet. The big doors being locked, the child tries the small ones, creates petty interests for emotional and intellectual satisfaction, deriving pleasure from pitting his intelligence against law and order. The fact that these cases do well in schools where special attention is paid to sports and interesting occupations adds weight to the belief that the majority of delinquents are not born but made. It is also another reminder to interpret the personality picture only in the light of the particular circumstances.

# 8

---

# EXAMPLES

---

NOTE

The three examples chosen to illustrate the process of scoring and interpretation of Rorschach records represent types that one meets in everyday life. Had these men not been drawn into the war and exposed to battle stress they would in all likelihood have led a normal existence without ever coming for psychiatric observation. The choice fell upon two personalities of the 'simple' type, because these form the bulk of our population, and one of the 'rich' type, because these are more vulnerable and therefore more often seen in the psychologist's consulting room. Reproduction of the tabulation has been omitted.

## EXAMPLE 1

| *Private X*, age 29, Service 10 months. | 1st March 1945. |
|---|---|
| Casualty Group: Battle Exhaustion. | Time: 11.18–11.37. |

### I

| 1. | 3″ | ∧ It looks like a bat. | | WF AP |
| 2. | | ∨ Could be leaves as well. | | WF— Veg. |
| 3. | | > —Or a map. | 11.19 | WF— Map |

### II

| 1. | 6″ | ∧ This part could be a butterfly (bottom red). | | DF AP |
| 2. | | ∧ Or a shell. (Subsequent inquiry: a shell going off.) | 11.20 | DCm Explos. |

138

### III

| | | | |
|---|---|---|---|
| 1. | 3″ | ∧ The middle one looks like a butterfly again (central red). | *DF AP* |
| 2. | | ∧ The ones up there (top reds) like a seal. | *DF A* |
| 3. | | ∧ These here (detached 'legs') look like crabs' legs. | *DF Ad* |
| 4. | | ∨ Almost like part of the body—a robot.  11.22 | ~~W~~*F H* |

### IV

| | | | |
|---|---|---|---|
| 1. | 6″ | ∧ Well, this looks like an animal skin. | *WF A/Obj.* |
| 2. | | ∧ The middle part (lower medial *D*) looks like an animal's head. | *DF Ad* |
| 3. | | ∧ A pair of boots (lateral *D*).  11.23 | *DF H/Obj.* |

### V

| | | | |
|---|---|---|---|
| 1. | 1″ | ∧ That again looks like a bat. | *WF AP* |
| 2. | | ∧ Or a rabbit, the middle one. | *DF AP* |
| 3. | | ∨ The side pieces look like a buffalo— with tail and rear legs. | *DF Ad(P)* |
| 4. | | > This looks like the beak of a bird (lower central spikes).  11.25 | *dF Ad* |

### VI

| | | | |
|---|---|---|---|
| 1. | 8″ | ∧ That looks like the skin of an animal again. | *WF A/Obj.* |
| 2. | | ∧ —And could be a flower at the top. | *DF Veg.* |
| 3. | | > That (upper part without fringes) has the appearance of a snake's head.  11.28 | *dF Ad* |

### VII

| | | | |
|---|---|---|---|
| 1. | 3″ | ∧ Well, that looks like a map—of mountains and valleys. | *Wk Map* |
| 2. | | ∨ Still get the butterfly effect on the top part (bottom *D*). | *DF A* |
| 3. | | ∨ Those little bits look like ice, falling (icicles, inner, upper edge).  11.29 | *ddm Ice* |

### VIII

| | | | |
|---|---|---|---|
| | | —Oh, that's a pretty one! | Exclam. |
| 1. | 8″ | ∧> These look like rats to me (lateral pink). | *DF AP* |
| 2. | | ∧ The middle part looks like a skeleton of sorts (central ribs). | *DF Anat.* |
| 3. | | ∨ The top part could be a dress (orange pink). | *DF H/Obj.* |
| 4. | | ∧ The top part (blue-grey) could be a tree of some kind.  11.31 | *DF Veg.* |

## IX

| | | | |
|---|---|---|---|
| 1. | 15″ | ∧∨ Oh, that looks like a part of the body—more of an X-ray (central streak). | dk Anat. |
| 2. | | ∧ These look like antlers (orange). | dF Ad |
| 3. | | > The pink looks like a man's profile. | DF HdP |
| 4. | | > Some look like clouds—(Later)—Like someone kneeling down. 11.33 | DK (M) Cloud |

## X

| | | | |
|---|---|---|---|
| 1. | 13″ | ∧> That one (lat. blue) looks like a crab to me. | DF AP |
| 2. | | ∧ Lots of them could be insects. | DF— A |
| 3. | | ∨ The middle ones look like Donald Duck (cent. bl.). | DF A |
| 4. | | ∧ There's a rabbit's head (bottom green). | DF AdP |
| 5. | | ∧ These could be petals of a flower—daffodils (lat. yellow). | D FC Veg. |
| 6. | | ∧ The green could be leaves (upper green). | D CF Veg. |
| 7. | | ∨ The red I could put down as petals—rose or poppy (pink). | D CF Veg. |
| 8. | | ∨ These two look like two animals that climbed to the top of a pole. 11.37 | D FM A |

Preference: Card X (It's more of an assortment; you can see more in it).
Dislike: Card IV (It's a bit fantastic).

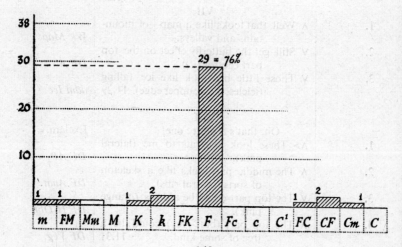

# Examples

Approach: $W=20\cdot5\%$; $D=65\cdot5\%$; $d=11\cdot5\%$; $dd=2\cdot6\%$; $\underline{W-D-d-dd}$.
Succession: loose.
$\Sigma F=76\%$; $F+=O$; $F-=10\%$; $(FK+F+Fc)=76\%$.
$A=49\%$; $P=26\%$; $O=0\%$; $Z=$ ordinary: $(H+A):(Hd+Ad)=13:8$.
$M:\Sigma C=0:3\cdot5$; $(m+FM):(K+k+FK)=2:2$; $(K+k+FK):$
$\qquad (\Sigma C+\Sigma C')=2:0$;
$W:M=8:0(1)$; $W:(m+FM+M+K)=8:3$; last three cards $=42\%$.
Colour preference: blue and green.

| Signs of Shock | | Signs of Neurosis | | Signs of Hysteria | | Intellectual Level |
|---|---|---|---|---|---|---|
| $T$ delay | : $+$ | $R<25$ | : $-$ | | | |
| $R$ lowered | : $(+)$ | Rejection | : $-$ | | | Number + qual. of |
| | | | | | | $W$: 6 fair, 2 poor |
| Qual. ,, | : $(+)$ | Col. shade: | $+$ | | | Number + qual. of |
| | | | | | | $M$: only trend to 1 |
| | | | | | | (poor) |
| Content | | | | | | |
| poor | : $+$ | $K$ | : $+$ | | | Number of $F$: 26 |
| $P$ failure | : $-$ | $FC<2$ | : $+$ | | | Number of $F+$: 0 |
| Order dis- | | | | | | |
| turbed | : $+$ | $M<2$ | : $+$ | | | Number of $F-$: 3 |
| Rejection | : $-$ | $FM>M$ | : $+$ | | | Number + qual. of |
| | | | | $F\%$ low | : $-$ | $O$: nil |
| Exclama- | | | | At least 1C: | $+$ | |
| tion | : $+$ | $F>50\%$ | : $+$ | Dilatation | : $-$ | Variety of content: |
| Comment | | | | $CF>FC$ | : $+$ | fair |
| on col. | : $-$ | $A>50\%$ | : $-$ | $\Sigma C>M$ | : $+$ | Succession: loose |
| Colour shy | : $-$ | Neur. | | $FM>M$ | : $+$ | (Abnormalities): $++$ |
| | | content | : $+$ | | | |
| | 4–6 | | 7 | | 3 | |

## CLINICAL INFORMATION ON THE CASE

Battle exhaustion case; gun-shy and very apprehensive. Gives impression of being dazed. On the seventh day in action a grenade fell close by and blew his friend's face off. Sent out of line with uncontrollable shaking. Relevant history: parents separated. In childhood afraid of dark and slept with light. Poor school record. Worked as ironmonger's assistant. Happily married for two years, no children.

*The graph* shows a trend towards constriction: an attempt at outward control over his emotional tendencies, a restriction of spontaneity. *Basic Personality:* strongly extratensive. *Mental Activity:* the

141

approach is pretty average ('normal'). The proportion of $W : M$ points to mental inactivity. A man who accepts the world without asking questions. Phantasy life is on a childish level—only one mere indication of a human pose; he is not equipped for mental creation or deep thought, and incapable of clear insight. *Intellectual level:* of the $W$'s three-quarters are average, one-quarter poor, of $M$ there is only an immature trend—suggestive of a mental age of nine; there are no $F+$ to balance three $F-$, and Originality is nil. This also points to a subnormal I.Q. Variety is fair, but below I.Q. 100; succession is loose. But the record is constricted and there are neurotic signs, so that an estimate of 75 would be too low for his I.Q., and a 10 per cent allowance for neurotic trends gives an I.Q. of 85–90, which is probably pretty near the mark, since he did not reach the top form of the elementary school.

## EMOTIONAL LIFE

### 1. Ties with Outer Reality

Emotionally unstable and impulsive ($CF$), he has a certain degree of social adaptation expressed mainly in conventional behaviour ($FC$). But he is liable to lose his head under stress ($Cm$), more likely in a passive form, such as a hysterical paralysis, or fainting, or fugue states (because of the combination of $C$ with the introversive factor $m$, a primary or hostile inner force). He is capable of enjoying life in a simple way and likes to be active (confirmed by his explanation that he could never sit still for long). The 'last three cards' percentage' shows that he is easily influenced by his environment.

### 2. Ties with Inner Life

One look at the graph shows that the mature mental powers ($M$) are lacking which should cope with an impulsive emotional life. The latter will stir up the primitive and immature drives ($FM$) which fill the main phantasy, and the dark, hostile inner drives ($m$). This agrees with the intellectual aspect: the man is not endowed with the mental faculties necessary for insight and purposeful control of emotion. His reaction to emotional stress will therefore be of a primitive order.

## OTHER FACTORS

Total $R=38$, Total Time 19 minutes, average $2R$/minutes, which suggests a facile power of association; would also go with a mildly hypomanic disposition and agrees with the $C$ observations on activity. The restrained turning confirms the superficial ease with which the responses were made, and their quality is in accord. His attitude towards the test is expressed in the wording of his responses and shows that he understood the nature of the task and entered into its spirit without worrying about results. His predilection for the edge of the blot tallies with his superficial attitude to life. He is definitely not a brain worker, and best fitted for semi-skilled work entailing physical activity.

## ABNORMALITIES

The graph shows the result of those inner drives which are not absorbed and sublimated by a mature phantasy: $K$ reveals inner anxiety, and $k$ points here to a certain amount of conscious depression, since insight is poor. Among the content is an 'explosion' ($II_2$), a frequent association with traumatic memories of shelling and bombing. There are two anatomy responses (concern with health): he is worried about possible injury.

Signs of shock are not very convincing, but Card II has obviously stirred painful memories. Signs of neurosis, however, are represented by all the most important factors except rejection. Signs of hysteria are not positive here but they suggest a likelihood of hysterical lack of control under stress.

*Content analysis* produces no fresh features but confirms the general impression of a mentally superficial personality of lower average intelligence.

## DIAGNOSTIC SUMMARY

An extratensive personality of lower average intelligence who is suffering from an anxiety state due to reaction of his uncontrolled emotions to battle stress. A type who could easily go through civilian life without breaking down, provided he is in a job he can cope with.

## The Rorschach Test

Example 2

*Sgt. Y*, age 40, Service 5 years      Date: 7th March 1945
Casualty Group: Battle Exhaustion.      Time: 3.54–4.20.

### I

| | | | |
|---|---|---|---|
| 1. | 83″ | ∧∨∧>∧∨ —No, sir, I can't make any-thing out of it. . . . (Encouraged) —it's this shape here (central fig.). —(Yes?)—well, it's like a human figure. | (Rejection) *dF H* |
| 2. | | ∧ And the whole thing I should say is like a photograph of a human backbone. | *Wk Anat.* *Phot.* |
| Add | | ∨ There's something I notice here (cent. white): these two are not ex-actly the same.     3.58 | *(S F descr.)* |

### II

| | | | |
|---|---|---|---|
| 1. | 22″ | ∧>∧ These two give you the impression of two men kneeling down look-ing away from you. Clapping hands. | *WM+ HP* |
| 2. | | > This here (up. edge lat. of 'spear head') looks like the outline of a face to me. . . . 'fraid I can't . . . (slants card at vari-ous angles). | *ddF Hd* (Remark) |
| 3. | | ∨ This part here seems to be some sort of a lampshade: | *SF Obj.* |
| 4. | | > I should say that that (top red) repre-sented a foot or a sock. | *DF Hd* |
| 5. | | <> To look at it that way you'd say it was a bear (lat. half of black).   4.02 | *DF A* |

### III

| | | | |
|---|---|---|---|
| 1. | 70″ | ∧>∨∧<∧ That one there seems like two waiters bowing, with hands at their sides. | *W̶M HP* |
| 2. | | ∧ And these here look as if someone were pointing a finger (detached 'legs') | *DMm Hd* |
| 3. | | > And that one there resembles a horse, I should say.    4.05 | *DF A* |

### IV

| | | | |
|---|---|---|---|
| 1. | 13″ | ∧ If I'd done it I'd say I did a poor job skinning a dingo. | *WFc A/Obj.* |
| | | ∨>∧<∨> I'm afraid that's all I can make out of this one.    4.07 | |

## Examples

### V

| 1. | 22″ | ∧∨∧ This one just looks like a bat—in flight. | WFM AP |
|---|---|---|---|
| 2. | | ∨∧ This here looks like sugar tongs (middle bottom spikes). | dF Obj. |
| | | ><∧ —No, I think that's about all in this one.     4.09 | |

### VI

| 1. | 52″ | ∧>∨∧< First thing, looking at the outline: it's a face here (lat. edge). | ddF Hd |
|---|---|---|---|
| 2. | | And a face there (lower down).    4.11 | ddF Hd |

### VII

| 1. | 17″ | ∧>∨∧< If you were looking at a Walt Disney cartoon, you'd say this was a dog, and this another (top and mid. D each side). | DF A |
|---|---|---|---|
| 2. | | ∨ This roughly represents a helmet with the camouflage (cent. white).   4.13 | SF H/Obj. |

### VIII

| 1. | 11″ | ∧> The idea is more or less a hyena I should say (lat. pink). | DF+ AP |
|---|---|---|---|
| 2. | | <∨>∧∨ This here (orange pink) more or less represents somebody kneeling with a cloak over their head. (Inquiry: engaged in some activity.)   4.15 | DM+(Fc) H |

### IX

| | (60″) | ∧>∨<∧>∨ No, I'm afraid I can't make out anything of this one, sir. | |
|---|---|---|---|
| | (+45″) | ∧<∨<∧ (Continues to turn the card)— No, sir.    4.17 | Rejection |

### X

| 1. | 100″ | ∧>∨<∧>∨<∨ There's only one here: the outline of a face here (lower lat. edge of pink). | ddF Hd |
|---|---|---|---|
| 2. | + | ∨ This here (top grey) looks like the stem of a flower with the petals all off after the stem has been cut. 4.20 | DF Veg. <br> Morb. |

Preference: X ('For the colouring'), ('But as a picture I prefer the dingo skin,' IV).

Dislike: III ('Don't know why—has a sort of . . . I've seen these things in my dreams lately. And this one (II) is the same sort').

Attitude: Heavy effort to co-operate, slow, but anxious to perform well.

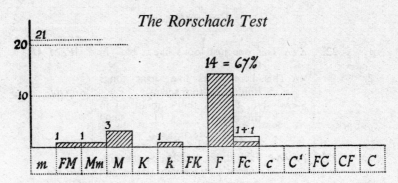

Approach: $W=24\%$; $D=38\%$ $d=10\%$; $(dd+S)=28\%$; $W-(D)-d-dd+S$
Succession: Loose.
$\Sigma F=67\%$; $F+=7\%$; $F-=0\%$; $(Fk+F+Fc)=71\%$.
$A=29\%$; $P=19\%$; $O=0$; $(H+A):(Hd+Ad)=9:7$.
$M:\Sigma C=3\cdot5:0$; $(FM+m):\Sigma K=1:1$; $\Sigma K:(\Sigma c+\Sigma C')=1:0\cdot5$. Last
    three cards 19%.
$W:M=4\cdot5:3\cdot5$; $W:(m+FM+M+K)=4\cdot5:4\cdot5$.

| Signs of Shock | | Signs of Neurosis | | Signs of Hysteria | | Intellectual Level |
|---|---|---|---|---|---|---|
| T delay | : — | R<25 | : + | | | |
| R lowered | : — | Rejection | : + | | | Number and qual. of W:1 good, 4 fair, average |
| Qual. „ | : — | Col. shade | : — | | | Number and qual. of M: 2 good, 2 fair (1WM+) |
| Content poor · | : — | K+shading shock | : + | | | Number of F: 13 |
| P—failure | : (+) | FC<2 | : + | | | Number of F+ :1 |
| Order disturbed | : — | M<2 | : — | F% low | : — | Number of F—: 0 |
| Rejection | : + | FM>M | : — | Dilatation | : — | Number and qual. of O: (tendency to Obj.) |
| Exclamation | : — | F>50% | : + | At least 1C :— CF>FC | : — | Variety of content: fair |
| Comment on col. | : — | A>50% | : — | ΣC>M | : — | Succession: loose |
| Col. shy | : (+) | Neur. content | : (+) | FM>M | : — | (Abnormality: 1 Anat. k trend) |
| | 1 | | 5–6 | | 0 | Above average, below Scholarship: I.Q. 100–105 |

# Examples

## CLINICAL NOTES

Admitted from battle zone with acute headache, insomnia, and depression. Very gun-shy and apprehensive but not tremulous.

Had been in heavy action for seven months (tanks) and not turned a hair after being blown out of his tank on two occasions. Broke down on return from adventurous forty-eight hours' mission when he had to drive over the dead bodies of his men through a lane in a minefield.

A lean-flanked, broad-shouldered tough, whose childhood and family background had been outwardly normal, and whose restless urge for adventure drove him all over the globe. He had in turn been blacksmith, gold digger, cattle rustler and snake hunter. He had enlisted at the outbreak of war and soon got his stripes. He had a good reputation in his unit and cared for the welfare of the men in his charge. As ward N.C.O. he is a mixture of drill sergeant, daredevil, and father of the poor.

## BASIC PERSONALITY

The graph suggests a completely introvert type, a possible daydreamer ($M$ and $W : M$). The clinical notes contradict such a conception emphatically: he has been a hypomaniac possibly of a schizoid kind, all his life, and is now suffering from a depression. It is therefore justifiable to assume that the $M : C$ ratio is not the picture of the basic personality but of a depressive process of the manic-depressive or cyclothymic type, though not necessarily psychotic in origin. The relative constriction ($F=67$ per cent) and the $k$ support this view. The basic personality picture has therefore been obliterated by an acute depressive change. The Approach is singularly expressive of the man's tendency to forgo all common sense in the hunt for trifles. He has a normal aptitude for the abstract, but he lacks that practical sense which should mediate between lofty ideals and petty interests. That tallies admirably with his career as an adventurer and supports the belief that the present depression is the cause of the loss of a good many $FC$ and $CF$ responses which had once been present. (Comp. with note on juvenile delinquency, p. 137.)

## MENTAL ACTIVITY

His phantasy is in excess of his creative output ($W : M=4.5 : 3.5$). The graph reveals no outlet, so that it must be assumed that he could quite likely be obsessed with disturbing phantasy pictures in his

K*
147

depression. (Actually he thinks and dreams of the dead boys of his platoon, over whose bodies he had to drive.)

His *Intelligence Level* is somewhat above normal, approximately I.Q. 100–105, which is no advantage when there is no steadying and guiding power to harness his intelligence.

## EMOTIONAL LIFE
### Ties with Inner Life

Phantasy life has absorbed whatever there had been. (Total lack of colour responses.)

## OTHER FACTORS FOR INTERPRETATION

Total time for twenty-one responses is twenty-six minutes—too long for a normal average, and suggestive of a slowing of faculties. His general attitude towards the test expressed this retardation in his effort to co-operate. Turning is excessive, but usually only for the first response: once he has adjusted himself towards the blot and become familiar with it, the gates are open. There is no facile, rapid association as in the case of the previous example. But he avoids pondering about problems and analysing them; he prefers the day-dream to philosophic abstraction and in his present condition the day-dream has turned nightmare.

## ABNORMALITIES

The excess of $M$, total absence of $C$, the high $F$ percentage, the $k$; signs of shock are practically absent—but the rejection of IX increased the significance of the factors of neurosis. It is not fully convincing, however, because two important signs are missing, '$M<2$' and '$FM>M$'. The symptoms are not only due to a neurotic process. All signs of hysteria are completely lacking, there can only be one other explanation in a man of his intelligence: the presence of an endogenous factor. This agrees with the experience that a shift from extratensive to introversive is particularly common in the manic-depressive and cyclothymic temperaments, the type which one is dealing with here.

## CONTENT

This reveals an abnormal concern with the human figure accompanied by emotional reactions. Card I is nearly rejected because he will not allow himself to become conscious of the central figure, which promptly leads to an anatomy response and then an escape into $S$. In

## Examples

II he rises to the occasion with a *WM* but is obviously upset (the men look away from him), finds no peace in a *ddF, Hd* and once more flies into *S*. In III the bowing waiters are followed by a 'pointing finger', which could almost score the psychopathic *m*, but is fortunately too large a detail and more than only the finger, since he refers to the whole of that detached mass, not only to its point. In IV the idea of the skinned dingo seems to stop further responses. In VI a couple of small faces are his total output. In VII the second and final response is to the white space 'a soldier'; in VIII the human being hides under a cloak; IX is rejected after much effort; X starts with a *dd* face, and ends in a symbolic death. Note also how he expresses preference for Card X, which took 100 seconds for the first response, and for IV which elicited only a simple one. His dislike for Cards II and III, the ones which he gave most responses to, leads to a belated recognition of the connection between his human responses and his nightmares.

## DIAGNOSTIC SUMMARY

A reactive depression in a cyclothymic personality of good intelligence, combined with an anxiety state. Basic personality of the potential delinquent type, probably with schizoid tendencies. A man who could achieve success if a dominant force or interest kept him steadily at his job.

### EXAMPLE 3

*Mr. Z, age 25, Clerk*          Time: 11.21–12.00.
*Civilian Case.*

#### I

| | | | |
|---|---|---|---|
| 1. | 30″ | ∧∨ Collision, sir. Plane hitting a bridge. Pieces flying.    11.21 | *Wm Obj.:*   *War O* |
| 2. | | ∧∨ There is the impression of something reaching out to grip something (top claws).    11.24 | *dMm Hd* |

#### II

| | | | |
|---|---|---|---|
| 1. | 12″ | ∧ Get the impression of something beautiful—touched by warmth. | *WCc Abstr. O* |
| 2. | | ∧ And in the foreground clouds. | *KK Cloud* |
| 3. | | ∧∨ Certain amount of beauty from the centre, but I can't make it out. | *SF— Abstr.* |
| 4. | | ∨ The top red (=bott. red) has connection with the other reds, like flames from a burner.    11.27 | *DCm Fire* |

149

## III

| | | | |
|---|---|---|---|
| 1. | 30″ | ∧ (Laughs)—I want to consider this—a struggle or disagreement between two figures about a vase or something. | ~~W~~M HP |
| 2. | | ∧ The red tends to give the impression of temper. | DC symb.; Abstr. O |
| 3. | | ∧ The other splash of red might almost be taken for a butterfly—or a sort of peace bringer, splitting the figures and the design. | DF(m) AP, Abstr. O |
| 4. | | ∨ I get the impression of a conductor wearing a very vivid bow tie. | WM, FC, HO |
| | Add: | I get the feeling as if someone struck a wrong note and spoilt a composition of music.   11.30 | (Confab.) |

## IV

| | | | |
|---|---|---|---|
| 1. | 56″ | ∧∨∧ Suggestion of brute force, a tremendous figure squashing something down, an impression of impact, of shock—I'm afraid I can't get anything else from this.   11.32 | WM(m) H, Schiz. Abstract, O |

## V

| | | | |
|---|---|---|---|
| 1. | 120″ | ∧∨∧ Get the impression of an effeminate affair, these legs coming down (bott. cent. spikes) | dF Hdx |
| 2. | | ∧ And the reflection of a windmill in front of a pond, with gorse bushes on either side and flat country. | WFK, Landsc. O |
| 3. | | ∨ Gives the impression of some object being split, and that object giving off two columns of smoke.   11.38 | WKm Smoke O |

## VI

| | | | |
|---|---|---|---|
| 1. | 28″ | ∧∨ A lift. A shaft going down a coal mine. | Wk, Landsc. |
| 2. | | ∨ The grey gives a certain amount of depression you would get going down a mine and the black line a sort of being shut in. It gives the impression of a dividing line between life and death. | dK, Abstr. O<br><br>Abstr. and conf. |
| 3. | | ∧ And this way a thing of rare beauty—like an old candlestick. | DFc Obj. |

150

# Examples

| | | | |
|---|---|---|---|
| 4. | | ∧ Or a knife with a beautifully carved handle. But a fire has blotched it all out.  11.40 | *WKm Fire, Schiz.* |

### VII

| | | | |
|---|---|---|---|
| 1. | 5″ | ∧∨ I can see a set of four figures—head and shoulders of two and two. | *DF Hd* |
| 2. | | ∨ And then there is a background of two figures dancing. The whole impression is happiness, laughing. | *WM HP, Abstr.* |
| 3. | | ∧∨ And this way two women waking up at each end of the bed and looking at each other in amazement, hair standing up.  11.43 | *WM+ HP* |

### VIII

| | | | |
|---|---|---|---|
| 1. | 56″ | ∧∨∧ I get the impression of something Chinese from the colours; a pagoda. | *WFC(CF) Arch.* |
| 2. | | ∧ The head of some symbolic figure—a god—and two workmen cleaning it. The col. doesn't convey anything. | *WM H* Com. on col. |
| 3. | | ∨ I still get the impression of Chinese like a bridge (grey) and the bent, hanging over shape (or pink). | *WFm Landsc.* |
| 4. | | ∨ The red and orange give the impression of harmony and peacefulness, which is spoilt and cut off by the bluey-grey. | *WC Abstr. Schiz.* |
| 5. | | > This way, the impression of a frog leaping (lat. pink). | *DFM AP* |
| 6. | | > And the reflection in the water.  11.49 | *DKF Water* |

### IX

| | | | |
|---|---|---|---|
| 1. | 105″ | ∧∨∧—∨ A fountain of sorts. | *WKm Water* |
| 2. | | ∨ A red vapour going in, and the green vapour coming out on either side. | *WCm Cloud* |
| 3. | ++ | ∧ I get the impression of something very beautiful, with two very small figures at the bottom. | |
| 4. | | ∧ Drawing attention to it (small medial white space). They are coming out of the green cloud, and red gives warmth to it. Seems to stand for something very important. | *sM H* *DC symb. Abstr.* |
| Add: | | It's like jade. | *(Dc Obj. O)* |

151

| | | | |
|---|---|---|---|
| 5. | | ∧ It's like coming to a clearing in a forest, with a beautiful monument showing. | *WFK Landsc.* |
| 6. | | ∧ And two figures—guardians, guides, showing its beauty. | *DM H* |
| 7. | | ∧ The orange gives me the impression of sunset. | *DC symb. Sky* |
| 8. | | ∧ And the green the forest and the red the clearing. 11.54 | *DC Landsc.* |
| | | X | |
| 1. | 32″ | ∧∨ I think I could find a million things in this. The first is a Walt Disney face of a dog surrounded by abstract things. It gives the impression of beauty. | *WF Ad O* *(Abstr.)* |
| 2. | | ∧ And this way a castle stuck on a hill (top grey). | *DF Arch.* |
| 3. | | ∧ The (lat.) blue gives me the impression of some force of power attacking the castle with weapons, the green. | *DM(m) Abstr.* |
| 4. | | ∧ And the yellow and grey (lateral) gives me the impression of a sneaking attack. | *Dm Abstr.* |
| 5. | | ∧ And the red (lat. or.) of impending danger. But the castle seems to stand safe from it. | *DC Abstr.* |
| 6. | | ∧ And then again something Oriental: a man with slanting eyes and hands closed. | *WF+(Mm) HO* |
| 7. | | ∧ And then here (top grey), like a crown, very beautiful. | *DF Obj.* |
| 8. | | ∧ Being attacked by the blues and greens on either side, and all these (lat. y. and grey). | *Dm Obj. Symb.* |
| 9. | | ∧ The central blue gives me the impression of something impregnable, like faith, that cannot be touched. 12.00 | *DF(C. Symb.) Abstr.* |

Preference: X ('It seems something—if you lost a certain amount of faith in something, it would bring it back. That thing (central blue), unshakable, gives you confidence').
Dislike: IV ('A wave of aggression. Brute force abusing it').
Attitude: Keen artistic interest.

[1] To adjust the percentage of *W* and *D*, one *W̸* has been added to the *W*, the other to the *D* score. Such a division seems to be logical since the *W̸* response shows features of both.

# Examples

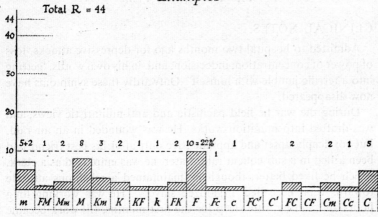

Total R = 44

Approach: $W=45\%$; $D=43\%$; $d=7\%$; $(dd+S)=4\cdot5\%$; $\underline{W}-(D)-(d)-S$

Succession: Methodical.

$\Sigma F=22\%$; $F+=10\%$; $F-=10\%$; $(FK+F+Fc)=29\%$.

$A=7\%$; $P=9\%$; $O=15\%$; $z=$unusual; $(H+A):(Hd+Ad)=11:4$.

$M:\Sigma C=9:9\ (m+FM):(\Sigma K+k+FK)=6:7; (\Sigma K+k+FK):(\Sigma c+\Sigma C')$
$=7:1\cdot5$.

$W:M=20:9; W:(m+FM+M+K)=20:31$. Last three cards $=52\%$.

| Signs of Shock | | Signs of Neurosis | | Signs of Hysteria | | Intellectual Level |
|---|---|---|---|---|---|---|
| $T$ delay | : — | $R<24$ | : — | | | |
| $R$ lowered | : — | Rejection | : — | | | Number and qual. of $W$: 3 good, 13 fair, Orig. 4 poor |
| Qual. „ | : — | Col. shock | : — | | | Number and qual. of $M$: 5 good, 3 fair, 2 poor |
| Content poor | : — | $K$ | : + | | | Number of $F$: 8 |
| $P$ failure | : + | $FC<2$ | : (+) | | | Number of $F+$: 1 |
| Order disturbed | : — | $M<2$ | : — | $F\%$ low | : + | Number of $F-$: 1 |
| Rejection | : — | $FM>M$ | : — | Dilatation | : + | Number and qual. of $O$: many abstract and schizoid |
| | | | | At least 1 C | : + | |
| Exclamation | : — | $F>50\%$ | : — | $CF>FC$ | : (+) | Variety of content: good |
| Comment on col. | : + | $A>50\%$ | : — | $\Sigma C>M$ | : — | Succession: method (good) |
| Col. shy | : — | Neur. content | : + | $FM>M$ | : — | (Abnormalities: many) |
| | 2 | | 2–3 | | 3–4 | |

153

## CLINICAL NOTES

Admitted to hospital two months ago for depressive attacks, loss of power of concentration, indecision, and, in his own words, 'getting into a terrific jumble with himself'. Outwardly these symptoms have now disappeared.

During the war he held pacifistic and anti-militaristic views, and was drafted into munition works. He was wounded in an air raid, but got deeply upset and apprehensive only after his best friend had been killed in a subsequent raid. Later, he was employed as a clerk, which he liked better, though he maintained a rebellious attitude towards what he called 'organized slavery'. He was working long hours and getting little sleep for the first months, till work became scarcer and he could relax. Reaction set in, and even a special rest period did not improve his condition, which deteriorated steadily till he was sent to hospital as a severe anxiety state.

He comes of good, middle-class stock; mother is suffering from headaches, otherwise family background and childhood normal. He was a good swimmer and boxer, left school at fourteen in the top class and studied commercial art at a well-known college.

Although an athletic type, he has always hated 'organized' life and split his existence into two separate entities, private and factory. As an artist he is unusually gifted, but recently his work has shown marked schizoid features which had not appeared before.

## BASIC PERSONALITY

A glance at the graph shows the dilated picture of a rich personality. There is rather too much spontaneity for his own good, and not enough control. $M : \Sigma C$ is 9 : 9, one of those ambivalent balances which are neither predominantly introversive nor extratensive, yet—particularly in this case—have powerful drives in both directions. Such people find life difficult.

If the graph is examined closer it will be seen that there are gaps in it which modify the first impression of richness. On the left-hand side the chiaroscuro responses cover almost the complete range of possibilities, but on the emotional side the surface-texture score is modest, while the black-white effects have escaped comment. It is also rather surprising that $CF$ responses are no more than indicated in the presence of so many and varied $C$ ones, considering the patient's athletic tastes. One feels inclined to make a note that he can't be as keen on physical activity as his build and earlier record would suggest, and observation confirms this. *CF* commonly goes with the urge to move with the whole body, while *FC* frequently accompanies the desire for manual activity. Here the picture suggests that the tremendous extratensive forces have found a catharsis of unusual character: sublimation in creative art. Most of his *C* responses are 'symbolics', and it is significant that he considers himself a black-white artist who does not express himself in a pure colour medium, yet feels the need of adding colour for decorative or symbolic purposes. Black-white is exclusively form-expression for him which accounts for his attitude towards possible *C'* interpretations.

The Approach suggests the idealist who lacks a good deal of common sense and an eye for practical matters. His considerations for the abstract are bound to interfere with his existence, particularly when the *S* factor, the opposition trend, is linked up with it. He is unorthodox in his tastes without being petty (total absence of *dd* and *ddd* forms), in fact, it would be better if he could see the stones and pebbles in his path before he stumbles over them. A man who lives with his head in the clouds. All that is needed now is to discover how good that head is, and how thick the clouds.

## MENTAL ACTIVITY

$W : M = 20 : 9 \ (19W + 2\cancel{W})$. There is creative ability far in excess of mental production. Mental creation ($W$) does not absorb all the mental (phantasy) drives, which will therefore need other outlets as well. There is too much phantasy and not enough clear abstraction. The 'head in the clouds' is therefore not a reliable guide for his steps. Lacking common sense and practical perception, he is at the mercy of more phantasy than is good for him. This becomes even more obvious in the proportion $W : (m + FM + M + K) = 20 : 31$; there are far too many inner drives which are not utilized. One suspects already that inner anxiety is absorbing a good many of them. $(H + A) : (Hd + Ad) = 11 : 4$ suggests that he is self-possessed and sure of himself.

## INTELLECTUAL LEVEL

This is very difficult to assess to any degree of accuracy, because there are too many abstract notions and flights of fancy involved. He is undoubtedly intelligent, but at the present moment he is not making the best use of his gifts. One can sense a good native intelli-

155

gence behind his responses. In view of his rather lop-sided mental development and the ambiguity of many responses, the potential rating should fall near I.Q. 105.

## EMOTIONAL LIFE

### 1. Ties with Outer Reality

Here he is spontaneous and very emotional. He feels deeply and passionately. Both his sensuality and his primitive (hostile) instincts are closely connected with his emotional reactions ($Cc$ and $Cm$), and reciprocal in their functions as primary instigators. His sensuality can lead to emotional outbursts and vice versa, as is also the case with his primitive drives; the problem of life and death for instance, can lead as easily to emotional reactions as the latter can give rise to thoughts of death. His social adaptation ($FC$) is quite inadequate in proportion to these emotional factors. He is incapable of adjusting himself to more than one milieu, and even within this one suspects that he cannot adapt himself fully. A mitigating circumstance is the fact that so many $C$ responses are symbolic, which points to an attempt to raise passion to a higher (abstract) level.

The last three cards' percentage (52 per cent) is high, and shows to what a great extent he is influenced by his environment.

### 2. Ties with the Inner Life

The crucial question is has he got enough mature phantasy to deal understandingly with all his emotional impulses? The answer here is, yes. But we have already seen (Mental Activity) that this phantasy life does not lead to enough mental creation, and therefore remains to a large extent on a phantasy level. The sublimation of his emotional life will therefore not take the form of a complete extension in mental creation, but a good deal will create phantasy pictures and be sublimated as art in a spontaneous, irrational form, or swell the bulk of inner anxiety. It will be bent on surrealist lines, portraying the interlacing chaos of many emotionally prompted ideas—that he cannot organize into clear thought.

The emotional overflow is stirring the hostile inner drives ($m$) and death fears will often rise to the surface.

## OTHER FACTORS FOR INTERPRETATION

The time factor is within normal limits. The general attitude helpful, and expressive of his mental preoccupation with art. Turning is restrained and after a good methodical survey (ΛVΛ) of the possibilities he starts by preference from the original position. He is not an analyst but impressionist in his method, and shows pronounced tendencies for synthesis and projection of his ideas into the blot. His *m* responses are mostly symbolic and superior, while his *C* responses are artistic with a leaning towards symbolism and abstraction. Both these points are in favour of a higher mental organization than is usually met with in cases where these reactions are powerful. The scarcity of *P* responses shows the unorthodox trend of mind, the contempt for the commonplace and the search for the original or unusual; Card V elicits none at all.

## ABNORMALITIES

There are a good many *K* responses. Neither the signs for shock nor for neurosis or hysteria give a positive answer. There is a good deal of emotional reaction and he is undoubtedly liable to states of depression if his inner anxiety makes itself more than usually felt. The content shows a few suspicious features like clouds and vapours, fire, and sunset. Its character is confabulatory with a tendency towards the schizoid, which is often associated with the predilection for abstract and symbolic responses. What is disturbing is the incidence of $F-$ in an otherwise good intelligence capable of producing $F+$, and the even $M : C$ balance.

## ANALYSIS OF THE CONTENT

This reveals a host of symbolic pictures which reflect on the inner turmoil. The problems of life and death, of world-order and violence, of emotional happiness and dismal distress, chase each other in wild profusion along a line traced by artistic perception. This content fits perfectly into the personality, endowed with a vivid phantasy yet unable to utilize all of it for creative, abstract thought—($W : M$). It fits the man who is led by superior ideals and abstractions while losing sight of the common-sense aspects of existence ($W : D : d : S$). It blends perfectly with what the graph shows. And, last but not least, it depicts the man as he is clinically. It would lead too far to discuss the content in detail; the reader will have no difficulty in interpreting it.

## DIAGNOSTIC SUMMARY

A richly, but somewhat unevenly, gifted personality, who is sublimating his powerful emotional impulses in his work as an artist as far as possible, but has not learned to use his mental energies to the full for that kind of creative thinking that might solve his inner problems. His powers of adaptation are limited, and he has broken down under conditions of life for which he was not equipped. He is opposed to restraint in any form. His ambivalence allowed him to lead a double existence—artist in phantasy, clerk in fact. There is little trace now of the depressive phase he is reported to have shown four months ago (*K* responses?) and which then left their mark on his work. Instead, there is a schizoid tendency with ominous lapses from *F*+ to *F*— and an ambivalent *Erlebnis Balanz*. Such a total configuration suggests the danger of a schizophrenic breakdown under unfavourable circumstances of existence.

Given guidance and opportunity he should, however, make a satisfactory adaptation to life as an artist and escape the danger of a more serious breakdown.

The 'Signs of hysteria' are very suggestive of a strong, hysterical element underlying his symptoms. In this personality one must therefore bear in mind that the onset of a Schizophrenic breakdown may be masked by symptoms of 'plain hysteria'.

# INDEX

*A* (see Animal responses)

Abstract, interest in, 95

  responses, 39, 45, 128

  thought, 97, 134

*Ad* (see Animal responses)

Additional responses, 27, 46

  significance of, 85

Adolescence, exclamations in, 87

  sexual conflict in, 88

  *W* responses in, 57

*Adx*, 130

Anatomy responses, 44

  sexual, 47

  significance of, 80

Animal objects, 44

Animal responses, definition, 43

  and intelligence, 102

  and movement (see Movement responses)

  in neuroses, 118

  percentage, 116

  ratio $(A+H):(Ad+Hd)$, 114

  significance of, 80

Anxiety, inner, 66, 67

Anxiety state (see Neuroses)

Artists, 68, 73, 77, 80

  *Cn* responses in, 113

Athletes, 79, 80

Awareness of emotional life, 75

Balance of Experience, 93

Beck, S. T., 7, 37, 124

Behaviour trends, 77

Bibliography, 6, 7

Binder, H., 7, 41

Bizarre responses, 28

Black and white as colour (see Pseudo-colour responses)

Blood, 38, 44, 61

  assessment of, 111

  and movement, 38, 61

  significance of, 82

Blots I–X, diagrams of, 31–4

'Burned child reaction', 76, 109

*C, CF* (see Colour responses)

*C/F*, 127

$C^1$, $C^1F$ (see also Pseudo-colour responses)

  ratio $(\Sigma C^1 + \Sigma c):(FM+m)$, 131

*c, cF* (see Surface-texture responses)

  ratio $(\Sigma c + \Sigma C^1):(FM+m)$, 131

Cards I–X, diagrams of, 31–4

Caves, 40

Chiaroscuro responses (see also *K, KF, FK, k*), 27, 39, 65

Childhood fixation, 85

Children, responses in, animal, 80

  confabulation, 85

  conflict, sexual, 88

  *ddd*, 41, 59

  *F descr:*, 45

  movement, 37, 62, 63, 64

  negative, 88

  question-form, 62, 87

  rejection, 89

  sexual conflict, 88

  succession, 103

  *W*, 57

  testing, 24, 78

Cloud, 38, 43, 44, 66, 111

*Cn* (see Colour naming)

Coarctation (see also Constriction), 93

Colour affinity, 105

  naming, 45, 111, 120

# Index

Colour affinity
  perception, 27
  responses, assessment of, 105
    combination with $K$, 128
      with $m$, 126
    definition, 42
    and emotional life, 77, 107
    *FC:CF:C*, ratio, 106
      in hysteria, 119
    *M:ΣC* ratio, 107
      in hysteria, 119
    *m+FM:* colour ratio, 108
    relation to Pseudo-colour responses, 75
    significance of, 76
    value of in assessment, 93
  shock, 85, 118
    signs of, 92, 115
  shyness, 117
  symbolic, 128
Comments, 23
  on colour, 117
Confabulation, assessment of, 113
  in children, 85
  definition, 46
  significance of, 85
Constriction of personality, 93, 101
Content, 43
Creation of ideas, 97, 98, 109
*C symb:*, 128

*D*, definition, 35
  diagrammatic outlines, 31–4
  significance of, 58
  with $S$, 125
*d*, definition, 36
  diagrammatic outlines, 31–4
  significance of, 58
  with $S$, 125
*dd*, definition, 36
  significance of, 58
*ddd*, definition, 36
  and movement, 64
  significance of, 58
Darkness, 39, 127
  and light, 127

Delinquents, 79, 137
  approach in, 96
Depressive states, 14, 67, 84, 89
  differentiation, 136
  *F%* in, 94
  time in, 111
Detail responses (see *D, d, dd, ddd*)
*Dr*, 125, 129
*DS*, 125
*dS*, 125

Earl, C. J. C., 8, 127
Emotional instability, 77, 78
  life, 77
  personality, 14
  repression, 76
Enuresis, 137
Environment, influence of, 77
Epilepsy, 136
*Erlebnis balanz*, 93
Exclamations, 23
  assessment of, 114
  definition, 47
  significance of, 87
Experience balance, 93
Explosions, 44, 111
Extratensive personality, 14, 93
  and *WM:* ratio, 98
Extravert, 93

*F, F+, F—* (see Form responses)
Falsification of response, 19, 28
*FC* (see Colour responses)
*F/C*, 127
*FC¹* (see Pseudo-colour responses)
*Fc* (see Touch-feeling responses)
Fire, 38, 44, 61, 82, 111
Fixations, 85, 96
*FK* (see Vista response)
*F/K*, 127
*FM* (see also Movement, animal)
  ratio $(FM+m):(Σc+ΣC^1)$, 131
Form-colour combinations, 127
Form-description, 45, 113
Form responses, 116
  assessment of *F+, F—*, 70
  definition, 40

# Index

Form responses
 F+ in relation to movement, 71
 and intelligence, 101
 percentage in neurosis, 118
 significance of, 69
Formulae, intelligence, 92
 colour-shock, 92
 neurosis, 92
 organic, 93
 hysteria, 93
Free anxiety (see Inner anxiety)

Garments, 44
Grained wood, 72
Graphs, 92, 94

H, Hd (see Human response)
Hdx, 130
Health, concern with, 80
Hesitation, 88
Homicide, 78, 114
Homosexual responses, 88
Hostile inner forces, 62, 98
Human-objects, 44
Human responses, definition, 44
 and movement (see Movement re-
  sponses, human and minor
  human)
 ratio (A+H):(Ad+Hd), 114
Hypochondria, 81
Hypomania, 84, 89, 111
Hysteria (see also Neuroses), 119
 Hertz' signs of, 119

Impotence, 120
Impressionistic responses, 127, 128
Inanimate movement (see also
  Movement, inanimate)
 definition, 38
 significance of, 61
Infantile fixations, 63
Inner anxiety, 66, 67
 forces, hostile, 62
 life, 107
Insight, 68
Instinctive drives, primitive, 63, 98
Intelligence, assessment of, 98

formula, 92
quotient, 98
Introversion, 93
I.Q., 98

Juvenile delinquency, 79, 137

K, assessment of, 112
 combination with C, 128
 c, 38, 128
 m, 38, 66, 126, 131
 definition, 39
 in intellectuals, 66
 in neurosis, 118
 significance of, 65
k, assessment of, 112
 definition, 39
 and m+Fm, 131
 significance of, 66
KF, 127
K/F, 127
Klopfer, B., 30, 41, 128
Klopfer, B., and Kelly, D. McG.,
 6

Last three cards, 49
 percentage, 83
Light and darkness combinations,
 127
Limits, testing, 46
 definition, 26
Literary gifts, 68
Love, 78

M (see Movement, human)
m (see Movement, inanimate)
Malingering, 19, 28, 89, 111
Mania, 111
Manic-depressive psychosis (see
 also Depressive states), 14, 136
Manual dexterity, 79
Maps, 40
 coloured, 127
 relief, 39
Marble, 72
Masochism, 85
Meat, 82

161

# Index

Medical profession, responses in, 80, 87

Melancholia (see Depressive states),

Mental approach, assessment of, 94
definition, 30
scoring variations from normal, 95
significance of, 56

Mental creation, 97, 98, 109

Mental defect, 80, 88, 89, 96, 113, 131, 136

Miale, F. R., and Harrower Ericksen, H. R., 92, 118

Microscopic enlargements, 39

Minute detail responses (see *ddd*)

*Mm* (see Movement, minor human)

Morbid responses, assessment of, 114
definition, 46
significance of, 85

Movement, combination with *K* and *C*, 38, 66
connection with *F*+, 71
perception of, 26

Movement responses:
Animal, and *C*¹, 131
and *c*, 131
definition, 38
and *K* ratio, 131
significance of, 62
Human, combination with animal, 64
definition, 39
significance of, 63
Inanimate, and *C*, 126, 131
definition, 38
and *K*, 126, 131
significance of, 61
Minor human, 64, 125
and intelligence, 99
proportion to colour responses, 93, 107
*W*, 97
ration *M:FM+m*, 98

Negative response forms, 87

Neuroses, 63, 80, 82, 88, 135

approach in, 96
*F%* in, 94, 119
formula, 92
obsessional, 135
rejection in, 114
sexual responses in, 88
signs of, 92, 118

Night, landscapes by, 127

Normal personality, 94, 133
graph and percentages, 92

Nurses, responses in, 80

*O* (see Original responses)

Oberholzer, E., 7

*Oligophrene Kleindetails*, 130

Obsessional neuroses, 135
personality, 59

Opposition, 60, 89

Ordinary responses, definition, 44

Organic brain lesions, 45, 111, 113, 131
reaction, signs of, 92, 119

Organizing talent, Beck's, 37, 124

Original responses, definition, 45
and intelligence, 120
significance of, 83

*P* (see Popular responses)

'*Pars pro toto*', response, 124

Pathognomic responses, 44, 111

Percentages, of *F* in neuroses, 118
tabulation of, 49
table of normal, 92

Perplexity, 120

Perseveration, 40, 120

Personality structure, 37, 61
graph and norms, 92

Perspective (see Vista response)

Phallic responses, 88

Phantasy, 61, 63, 64, 97, 98, 107
in adults, 63, 64
in children, 63
in delinquency, 137
in psychoses, 136

Photographs, 39

Piotrowski, Z. A., 92, 119

*Po* (see Position response)

# Index

Popular responses, 27
  in colour-shock, 116
  definition, 45
  diagrams and list of, 31–4
  significance of, 83
  and $W$, 99
Position responses, 129
Pseudo-colour responses, assessment of, 109
  definition, 42
  relation to Colour responses, 75, 109
  significance of, 74
Psychoses, 86, 88, 89, 135
  approach in, 96
  $Cn$ in, 113
  sexual responses in, 88

Question form of response, 47, 120
  assessment of, 111
  significance of, 87

$R$ (see Response total)
Rare responses, 36
  detail responses, 125, 129
Reality, reaction to, 77, 105
Record sheet, 22
Reflections, 40
Rejections, in colour-shock, 117
  definition, 25, 47
  in neuroses, 114, 118
  significance, 88
Remarks, assessment of, 114
  definition, 47
  recording, 23
  significance of, 87
Repression of emotion, 76
Response total, 27, 45, 83, 111, 118
  to coloured cards, 116
Re-tests, 19, 20
Rocks, 40, 44
Rorschach, H., 7, 13, 95, 115, 130
Rorschach Exchange Research, 7

$S$ (see Space response)
Sadism, 85

Schizoid personality, 63
  response, assessment of, 114
  definition, 47
  $F+F-$ sequence, 114
  significance of, 86
Schizophrenia, 86, 131
Scoring, 30
Sensuality, 72, 109
Sexual responses, 44
  assessment of, 111
  definition, 47
  in psychoses, 88
  significance of, 87
Shading shock, 118
  signs of, 92, 116
Shock (see Colour shock and Shading shock)
Smoke, 44, 111
Snow, 74
Social adaptation, 79
Space response, with $D$, $d$, 125
  definition, 36
  significance of, 59
  with $W$, 125
Spontaneous response, definition, 26, 70
  proportion of, 93
Spurting blood, 38, 61
Stubbornness, 60
Succession, 103, 116
  classification of, 104
Suicide, 78, 114
Surface pattern, definition, 41
  significance of, 71
  texture, combination with $K$, 128
  definition, 41
  significance of, 71
Symbolic colour, 128

Tabulation, percentages, 49
  sheet, 30
Tact, 72, 73, 109
Terman Merrill test of intelligence, correlation with, 99
Test procedure, 23
Testing for limits, 46
  description, 26

# Index

Time, average, 46, 50, 84
  for first response, 46, 84, 116
  total, 50, 111, 119
Touch-feeling, 27
  assessment of, 110
  definition, 41
  significance of, 71
Tulchin, S. H., 13
Turning, 23, 48
  assessment of, 111
  significance of, 89
Twins, testing uniovular, 19

Unusual details (see *ddd*)

Variety of content, and intelligence, 102
Vista response, 27, 67
  assessment of, 111
  definition, 39
  and *FM+m*, 131
  significance of, 68
Vocational advice, 108

*W*, 26

in adolescents, 57
assessment of, 97
in children, 57
definition, 35
and intelligence, 99
proportion to Movement responses, 97
significance of, 56
and Space responses, 125
definition, 35
significance of, 57
Water, 38, 42, 44
White and black as colour (see Pseudo-colour responses)
White space responses (see Space responses)
Whole-blot responses (see *W*)
*WS*, 125
*Wv*, 123
*W vulgär* (see *Wv*)

X-rays, 39, 44

*Z* (see Organizing talent)

*Note.*—Section headings set out in the Table of Contents, pp. 9–12, have not been repeated in the Index.